D0064813

372.7
D22

SDO

A COLLECTION OF PERFORMANCE TASKS AND RUBRICS: PRIMARY SCHOOL MATHEMATICS

Charlotte Danielson
and
Pia Hansen

Nyack College Library

EYE ON EDUCATION
6 DEPOT WAY WEST, SUITE 106
LARCHMONT, NY 10538
(914) 833–0551
(914) 833–0761 fax

Copyright © 1999 Eye On Education, Inc.
All Rights Reserved.

For information about permission to reproduce selections from this book, write: Eye On Education, Permissions Dept., Suite 106, 6 Depot Way West, Larchmont, NY 10538.

Library of Congress Cataloging-in-Publication Data

Danielson, Charlotte.
    A collection of performance tasks and rubrics: primary school mathematics / Charlotte Danielson and Pia Hansen.
        p.   cm.
    Includes bibliographical references and indexes.
    ISBN 1-883001-70-6
    1. Mathematics—Study and teaching (Primary)—Evaluation. I. Hansen, Pia, 1955– . II. Title.
    QA135.5.D244   1999
    372.7—dc21   98–51694
                                                                              CIP

10 9 8 7 6 5 4

Editorial and production services provided by
Richard H. Adin Freelance Editorial Services,
9 Orchard Drive, Gardiner, NY 12525 (914-883-5884)

40460026

Other Eye On Education Books on Mathematics Education

A Collection of Performance Tasks and Rubrics:
Middle School Mathematics
by Charlotte Danielson

Upper Elementary School Mathematics
by Charlotte Danielson

High School Mathematics
by Charlotte Danielson and Elizabeth Marquez

Bringing the NCTM Standards to Life:
Exemplary Practices From High Schools
by Yvelyne Germaine-McCarthy

Bringing the NCTM Standards to Life:
Best Practices From Elementary Educators
by Lisa B. Owen and Charles E. Lamb

Mathematics the Write Way:
Activities for Every Elementary Classroom
by Marilyn S. Neil

Teaching Mathematics in the Block
by Susan N. Gilkey and Carla H. Hunt

Other Eye On Education Books on Performance Assessment

Performance Standards and Authentic Learning
by Allan A. Glatthorn

Performance Assessment and
Standards-based Curricula:
The Achievement Cycle
by Allan A. Glatthorn with Don Bragaw,
Karen Dawkins, and John Parker

The Performance Assessment Handbook:
Volume 1: Portfolios and Socratic Seminars
Volume 2: Performances and Exhibitions
by Bil Johnson

FOREWORD

The *Curriculum and Evaluation Standards for School Mathematics* released by the National Council of Teachers of Mathematics (NCTM) has profoundly influenced the vision and practice of mathematics education. Through its call for a greater emphasis on problem-solving, reasoning, and communications, the *Standards* have validated the expanded use of performance tasks for classroom instruction and assessment. Effective performance tasks call for such reasoning and communication by engaging students in applying mathematical concepts and skills in the context of "authentic" problems.

While educators generally understand and support the recommendations of NCTM to incorporate performance tasks for assessment purposes, a number of practical questions remain: How do teachers develop "authentic" tasks to assess students' understanding, reasoning, and mathematical communications? How does the use of performance tasks fit with more traditional forms of assessment in mathematics? How do teachers evaluate student responses since performance tasks typically call for more than a single, correct answer?

Charlotte Danielson and Pia Hansen offer timely and practical answers in this readable guide to the development and use of performance tasks and rubrics in primary school classrooms. The book provides an excellent overview of the rationale for, and the strengths and limitations of, the use of performance tasks to assess student achievement and progress in mathematics. They offer a user-friendly, field-tested process for developing performance tasks and rubrics, along with practical advice for evaluating student work, selecting "anchors," and establishing performance standards. Finally, the sample tasks, rubrics and student work samples provide tried and true resources for immediate use, while serving as models to guide development of additional tasks and scoring tools.

Readers of *A Collection of Performance Tasks and Rubrics* will not be confronted with an ivory tower treatise on what should be. Rather, they will discover a valuable resource, grounded in the wisdom of years of experience in schools and classrooms, for making the NCTM vision come to life.

Jay McTighe
Director, Maryland Assessment
Consortium

PREFACE

Educators have recognized the unique role of assessment in the classroom environment for some time. Assessment provides valuable information for both teachers and students regarding how well each is doing. Students can see where they went wrong in their understanding and teachers can determine whether a concept needs to be retaught. Monitoring progress on valued learning goals is the first purpose of assessment, and one that supports every other purpose.

Assessment also defines what students must know and be able to do to succeed in a particular teacher's class. When teachers coach their students in how to prepare for a test, they are conveying what is important, both to them and in the subject. Such coaching can also serve a clarifying purpose for teachers. By specifying what their students should study in preparation for a test, teachers must confront their subject and make decisions about what is truly important. This is also true when teachers design the test.

However, there is much more to assessment than simply monitoring student progress and clarifying expectations. Because most tests "count," they also motivate students. That is, to the extent that tests or other assessments are used to calculate their grades, students will try to do well. Tests can "count" for teachers as well. In some towns, for example, scores on standardized tests are published in the newspaper; student scores on AP tests are seen as reflections on their teachers' instructional skills; and some states and school districts use test scores as the basis for teacher rewards or sanctions. When test scores matter, teachers attempt to have their students do well. And while few teachers engage in unethical practices, most teachers do provide instruction in such a manner as to assist their students in performing as well as they can.

But it is not only in defining the content that tests and other assessments influence practice. The form matters as well. That is, when students are asked (and know in advance that they will be asked) to answer a number of multiple-choice or short-answer questions, they tend to prepare in that manner, committing to memory that which they predict will be on the test. If deeper understanding is not required for the test, they may not strive to achieve it. If a question is ambiguous, they will seek to read the mind of the teacher, to determine the right answer even if they believe another is better.

The form of assessments affects teacher practices as well. If a test does not require or reward understanding, why should teachers emphasize it in their own classrooms? If all that is needed in mathematics, for example, is for students to get the right answer (possibly without understanding why the procedure works) then the procedure is all that will be provided in some classrooms.

Assessments matter, therefore, both in what they assess and in how they assess it. The content of a test affects what students study and what teachers teach, and the form of the assessment affects how they approach the task. Teachers have discovered, for example, that if they want their students to become better writers, they must make good writing count in the classroom; they must teach it systematically and assess it authentically. A test of correcting errors, for example, will not do; they must assess students' actual writing. Similarly, if teachers want students to acquire skills in solving mathematical problems or in communicating their mathematical ideas, they must both teach and assess those skills.

These considerations have provided much of the energy behind the movement toward performance assessment; that is, students actually creating or constructing an answer to a question. Teachers and policymakers alike have discovered that when assessment tasks more accurately mirror the types of learning goals they have for students—in both the content and the form of assessment—the learning environment is transformed. The assessments themselves tend to be motivational and engaging; students invest energy in the tasks and commit to them. In addition, performance assessments serve to educate as well as to assess student learning; teachers find that their students learn from doing performance tasks.

However, performance assessment has an enormous drawback; it is time-consuming to design and to work into classroom instructional time. Even teachers who are committed to the practice of performance assessment find that they don't have time to design good performance tasks, to try them out with students, and to perfect them for later use. Furthermore, most teachers did not learn to design performance tasks and scoring rubrics as part of their professional preparation. Although many educators have learned such skills as part of their continuing professional growth, many lack the confidence to use performance tasks as a central part of their assessment plan.

This book addresses this need. Because many educators are interested in incorporating performance assessment into their classroom routines, but either have not yet acquired the technical skill or do not have the time required to design them on their own, this book provides a collection of performance tasks and scoring rubrics for a number of topics in primary school mathematics. Teachers can use these performance tasks and scoring rubrics as is, or adapt them for their students and their particular situation. This book saves time for busy educators by providing examples of tested performance tasks. The samples of student work provide a range of responses that clarify the tasks and anchor the points on the scoring rubrics.

ABOUT THE AUTHORS

Charlotte Danielson, Program Administrator at Educational Testing Service, has consulted on performance assessment for numerous schools and school districts across the country and overseas. She is the author of *Enhancing Professional Practice: A Framework for Teaching* and *Teaching for Understanding,* both published by ASCD. She is also the author of two other volumes (and coauthor of another volume) in the series A Collection of Performance Tasks and Rubrics, published by Eye On Education.

Pia Hansen is a first–second grade, multiage teacher at Deming Elementary School. She has been the owner/director of a Montessori preschool/child care center for 10 years and has taught Kindergarten through third grade for the public schools in Cheyenne, Wyoming. Hansen is the 1997 Presidential Award Winner for Excellence in Mathematics Education from Wyoming. She facilitates classes for teachers in Primary Mathematics and Assessment.

TABLE OF CONTENTS

1

CLASSROOM USE OF PERFORMANCE ASSESSMENT

PERFORMANCE ASSESSMENT: AN OVERVIEW

This book concerns the classroom use of performance assessment and the evaluation of student work in response to performance tasks. It contains, as its heart, a collection of performance tasks in primary school mathematics; but it also includes guidance for educators on designing or adapting performance tasks.

While performance assessment is essential to a well-rounded assessment plan, it should not be used exclusively. Traditional testing has an important role to play, particularly to assess a large domain and to evaluate student knowledge. But to assess student understanding, to ascertain how well students can apply their knowledge, some type of performance assessment is essential.

In this book, "performance assessment" means any assessment of student learning that requires the evaluation of student writing, products, or behavior. That is, it includes all assessment except multiple choice, matching, or true/false testing. Classroom-based performance assessment includes all such assessment that occurs in the classroom and that is evaluated by teachers as distinct from, for example, large-scale, statewide performance testing programs.

Performance assessment is fundamentally criterion-referenced rather than norm-referenced. That is, teachers who adopt performance assessment are concerned with the degree to which students can demonstrate knowledge and skill in a certain field. They know what it means to demonstrate competence; the purpose of a performance assessment is to allow students to show what they can do. The criteria for evaluating performance are important; teachers use their professional judgment in establishing such criteria and in defining levels of performance. The standards teachers set for student performance are typically above that expected for minimal competency; they define *accomplished* performance.

Norm-referenced tests are less valuable than performance assessments to teachers. True, teachers may learn what their students can do when compared with other students of the same age, but the items on the test may not reflect the curriculum of a given school or district. To the extent that the curriculum is different, the information provided may have no value to the teacher. Moreover, the results of most standardized tests are not known for some time. Even for those items included in a school's curriculum, it does not help a teacher to learn in June that in April a student did not know a concept that was taught the previous November. Of what possible use is that information? It may not even still be true. And if true, it comes too late to be useful.

In addition, the only way for students to demonstrate progress on a norm-referenced test is to improve with respect to other students. Progress per se is not shown as progress. A student's standing may move from the 48th percentile to the 53rd percentile. However, the student may not have learned much; other students may have learned less! So while norm-referenced tests have their value—for example, for large-scale program evaluation—they are of limited use to teachers who want to know what their students have learned. Performance assessment, then, is criterion-referenced; it reflects the curriculum goals of a teacher, school, or district, and when used in the context of classroom teaching, it informs instructional decisions.

The remaining sections of this chapter describe the different types and uses of performance assessments.

SUMMARY

Classroom-based performance assessment is criterion-referenced and is used to evaluate student learning on clearly identified instructional goals. As such, it should be designed for optimal usefulness to its different audiences: teachers, students, and parents.

THE USES OF CLASSROOM-BASED PERFORMANCE ASSESSMENT

Assessment of student learning in the classroom can serve many ends. When teachers design their assessment strategies, it is helpful to determine, at the outset, which of the many possible uses is intended. Some possibilities are described here.

INSTRUCTIONAL DECISION-MAKING

After they have taught a concept, teachers discover that many students didn't "get it," that, while the students may have had looks of understanding on their faces and may have participated in the instructional activities, they are unable to demonstrate the knowledge or understanding on their own.

This is important information for teachers to have as they determine what to do next with a class or with a few students. They may decide that they must reteach the concept or create a different type of instructional activity. Alternatively, if only a few students lack understanding, a teacher might decide to work with them separately or to design an activity which can be used for peer tutoring.

Whatever course of action a teacher decides on, however, it is chosen on the basis of information regarding student understanding, which implies that the assessment strategies used will reveal student understanding, or the lack of it. And when used for instructional decision-making, it is the teacher alone who uses the information. The results of the assessment are not shared with students, nor are they used for grading. The assessment is solely for the teacher's benefit, to determine whether the instructional activities achieved their intended purpose.

FEEDBACK TO STUDENTS

Performance assessment (like any assessment) may also be used to provide feedback to students regarding their progress. Depending on how it is constructed, a performance task can let students know on which dimensions of performance they excel, and on which they need to devote additional energy. Such feedback is, by its nature, individualized; the feedback provided to one student will be very different from that provided to another if their performances are different. It is efficient for the teacher, however, because the important dimensions of performance have been identified beforehand.

COMMUNICATION WITH PARENTS

Actual student performance on well-designed tasks can provide parents with highly authentic evidence of their children's level of functioning. Many parents are skeptical of tests that they don't understand, and are not sure of the meaning of numbers, percentiles, and scalene scores. But student answers to an open-ended question are easy to understand, and can serve to demonstrate to parents their child's level of performance. Such samples of student work are highly beneficial for open houses, or parent conferences, to validate the judgments of the teacher.

Such indication of student performance is of particular importance if a teacher is concerned about a child, and wants to persuade a parent that action is needed. When confronted with the work of their own child, it is difficult for parents to question the commitment of the teacher in meeting that child's needs. Whether the work is exemplary and the teacher is recommending a more advanced placement, or whether it reveals poor understanding, having actual samples of student performance is invaluable to a teacher in making a case for action.

SUMMATIVE EVALUATION OF STUDENT LEARNING

Like any assessment strategy, a performance assessment may be used to evaluate student learning and may contribute to decisions regarding grades. Grading is complex issue that is addressed more fully in Chapter 8, but the results from performance tasks, like any assessment, can serve to substantiate a teacher's judgment in assigning a grade.

SUMMARY

Classroom-based assessment may be used for several different purposes. An overall assessment plan will take all desired purposes into account.

DIFFERENT TYPES OF
CLASSROOM-BASED ASSESSMENT

Assessment takes many forms, depending on the types of instructional goals being assessed, and on the use to which the assessment will be put. The major types are presented in table form (Figure 1.1), and are described in the following sections.

TESTS

Tests are listed as the first major column in Figure 1.1. They have always been (and will continue to be) an important method for ascertaining what students know and can do. When teachers decide to move to more authentic aspects of performance to evaluate student learning, they do not abandon tests. On the contrary, tests are used for those types of assessment for which they are well-suited (for example, for sampling knowledge), recognizing their substantial strengths as a methodology.

Tests are generally given to students under what we call "testing conditions," that is, conditions that ensure that we are actually getting the authentic work of individuals and that the experience is the same for all students. Testing conditions are:

FIGURE 1.1. FORMS OF ASSESSMENT

TEST		PRODUCT		BEHAVIOR	
Multiple Choice	Constructed Response	Written	Physical	Structured	Spontaneous

Adapted from a worksheet developed by the Maryland Assessment Consortium

♦ Limited time

Generally speaking, time for a test is strictly limited. Students must complete the test within a certain amount of time (frequently a class period, but sometimes more or less than that.) This provision ensures that some students don't devote far greater time to the assignments than others.

♦ Limited (often no) resources

Although there are exceptions to this rule (such as open-book tests), students taking a test are usually not permitted to consult materials as they work. An insistence on no additional resources rules out, of course, trips to the library while taking a test. This provision ensures that what students produce on the test reflects only their own understanding.

♦ No talking with peers or looking at others' papers

When taking a test, it is important that students produce their own work. Unless teachers adhere to this condition, they are never sure whether what they receive from an individual student reflects that student's understanding, or that of his or her friends.

In addition, tests are of two basic types: select and constructed response.

♦ Multiple-choice

In a multiple-choice test, students select the best answer from those given. True/false and matching tests are also included in this category.

♦ Constructed-response

In a constructed-response test, students answer a question in their own words. Open-ended questions on a test are constructed-response, as are essay questions. Short-answer items are technically constructed-response items (because the student supplies the answer), but because there is generally a single right answer, such items are a special case and share more characteristics with multiple-choice items in their scoring.

Of course, a single test may contain a combination of multiple-choice and constructed-response items. In fact, most tests do; they generally consist of some multiple-choice, true/false, short-answer, or matching items for a portion of the test and several essays for the remainder. The balance between these different types of test items varies enormously, by subject, grade level, and the preference of the teacher.

Students in grades K-3 have limited reading and writing skills and that makes the responsibility of accurate assessment more challenging for school districts and for the classroom teacher. Oral interviews with students about their work and anecdotal records with teacher observations of students applying mathematical skills, provide us with authentic developmentally appropriate assessment.

Some basic mathematical skills to observe are number recognition and one-to-one counting in kindergarten, addition and subtraction facts to 10 in first grade, addition and subtraction facts to 20 in second grade, and place value sense and multiplication of single-digit numbers in third grade.

From the earliest years, students need an opportunity to share multiple strategies with one another to allow them to grow mathematically and take another person's perspective.

PRODUCT

A product is any item produced by students that is evaluated according to established criteria. A product is a thing, a physical object, and is generally (but not always) produced by students outside of school time. Students may take as long as they want and need, and may consult books and speak with other people. Products may be one of two types: written or physical.

+ Written products

    A written product may be a term paper, an essay for homework, a journal entry, a drama, or a lab report. It is anything written by students, but that is not written under testing conditions.

♦ Physical products

A physical product may be, for example, a diorama, a science construction, a project in industrial arts, or a sculpture. Physical products are three-dimensional things that take up space.

Some projects done by students represent a combination of written and physical products. For example, most science fair projects consist of a physical construction of some sort, combined with a written description of the scientific principles involved.

Products are a rich source of information for teachers seeking to understand what their students know and can do. However, products have a significant disadvantage, which limits their usefulness for high-stakes assessment: authenticity. When a student turns in a project, the teacher has no way of knowing the degree to which the work reflects the student's own knowledge and understanding, or the degree to which the student's parents or older siblings might have assisted. For instructional purposes, most teachers encourage their students to obtain as much help as they can get; students are bound to learn more from an assignment with the insights of additional people. However, for purposes of assessment teachers need to know what each student can do; this requirement limits the usefulness of out-of-class assignments for evaluation. When used, such assignments should be supplemented by other sources of information (for example, an assignment given under testing conditions) where the teacher can be sure of authorship.

BEHAVIOR

Lastly, students demonstrate their knowledge or skill through their behavior, and this behavior can be evaluated. Behavior is that aspect of student performance which leaves no trace; once completed, it is finished. However, behavior may be captured, stored, and then evaluated. For example, a skit may be videotaped, a student reading aloud may be audiotaped. There are two types of behavior that may be used for evaluation:

♦ Structured behavior

With structured behavior, students are performing according to a preestablished framework. They may be staging a debate or a panel discussion. They may be giving a skit, performing a dance, or making a presentation. Teachers may be interviewing their students. Drama and speech classes depend on this type of performance to evaluate learning; it is useful in other fields as well.

♦ Spontaneous behavior

Students can also reveal their understanding through their spontaneous behavior. For example, their interaction when working on group projects, their questions during a discussion, and their choices during free time all demonstrate important aspects of their learning.

Because of the unstructured nature of spontaneous behavior, it is useful primarily as a supplemental form of assessment. However, for certain types of instructional goals, such as skill in collaboration, it may be the only appropriate form. Documenting spontaneous behavior depends on careful observation. Many teachers use checklists so that they can make their "kid watching" as systematic as possible.

SUMMARY

There are different important types of classroom assessment. The primary types of assessment include tests, products, and behavior. Their use depends on the instructional goals to be assessed, but they are all valuable. For the purposes of this book all types of assessment, except multiple-choice tests, are performance assessment.

2

WHY PERFORMANCE ASSESSMENT?

It is clear that the design and implementation of performance assessment are far more time-consuming than the use of traditional tests. Why, one might ask, should a busy educator go to the trouble of changing? A good question, and one that deserves a thoughtful answer.

When teachers use performance assessment, they don't stop using traditional forms of assessment. Tests will always be with us, and they should be. It is frequently important to know what students *know* about a subject; alternatively, we must be sure that they have read an assignment. There is no substitute for a quiz or a test to ascertain these things. But as a steady diet, tests have serious limitations, which are described in the following sections.

THE LIMITATIONS OF TRADITIONAL TESTING

By "traditional testing" we mean multiple-choice, true/false, matching, or short-answer tests that teachers create or adapt for use in their classrooms. These are generally provided by the publishers of text programs, or have evolved over time. Although they are useful for certain purposes (and they are certainly efficient to score), when used exclusively, they have a negative influence.

VALIDITY

The most serious criticism of traditional tests is that the range of student knowledge and skill they can test is extremely limited. Many aspects of understanding to which teachers (and their communities) are most committed simply don't lend themselves to multiple-choice assessment. Identifying the different categories of educational purposes (instructional goals) and considering how they can be assessed helps illustrate this point.

There are, of course, many different ways to classify goals for this type of analysis; one comprehensive classification scheme is outlined in the following material.

♦ Knowledge

Most types of knowledge, whether procedural knowledge (for example, how to wash lab equipment), conceptual understanding (for example, the meaning of buoyancy), or the application of knowledge (for example, determining the amount of paint needed to paint a room), may be assessed through traditional means. Indeed, it is in the assessment of knowledge that traditional assessment rightfully exerts its strongest influence.

However, conceptual understanding is not ideally suited to traditional testing because students can memorize, for example, a definition of buoyancy without really understanding it. Their lack of understanding might not be revealed through a multiple-choice or matching test. It is only through their explanation of the concept in their own words, or through their use of the concept in a problem that their understanding, or lack of it, is demonstrated.

♦ Reasoning

Traditional testing is poorly suited to assessing reasoning. While it is true that well-designed multiple-choice tests may be used to evaluate pure logic, most teachers without technical skills in this area are not advised to attempt it. Most of the reasoning we care about in schools (for example, analyzing data, formulating and testing hypotheses, recognizing patterns) is better assessed through alternative means.

♦ Communication

To know whether students can communicate, we must ask them to do so, in writing or by speaking. Attempts are made, of course, to evaluate students' understanding of written text and spoken language through multiple-choice tests. To some extent these attempts are successful; but they rarely give teachers information they did not already have through more informal means. For the productive aspects of communication—writing and speaking—there is no substitute for students actually writing and speaking, and then evaluating their performance.

♦ Skills

Social skills and psychomotor skills are completely unsuited to traditional forms of assessment. A multiple-choice test on the rules of basketball does not tell a teacher whether a student can dribble. A matching test on how to work in groups does not convey whether students have actually acquired skills in collaboration. Nothing short of observation will do, using a carefully prepared observation guide. To the extent that skills are important aspects of learning, teachers must employ nontraditional assessment methods.

♦ Affective Areas

As with skills, traditional testing is entirely un-suited to the assessment of the affective domain. To the extent that teachers attempt to cultivate students' productive dispositions towards work (for example, an open mind; pride in a job well done) they must look for little indicators through student behavior. As teachers try to cultivate an aesthetic sense in their students (for example, ap-preciation of the mood of a poem or the elegance of a mathematical proof), they must look for little comments and signs from their students. Other aspects of the affective domain are equally ill-matched to traditional testing, from self-confi-dence to traits such as honesty and respect for pri-vate property, through the ability to weigh ethical arguments.

As is evident from these descriptions, teachers using only traditional forms of assessment are unable to assess many as-pects (some would say the most important aspects) of stu-dent learning. Clearly, other assessment methods (construct-ed response tests, projects, and behavior) are needed. These alternative forms must be designed and procedures must be developed for the evaluation of the student work produced through them.

Design Issues

Measurement experts argue that most aspects of student knowledge and skill may be assessed through well-designed multiple-choice tests. They point to well-known tests that evaluate (they claim) problem-solving, reasoning, and data analysis. On further examination, by looking at the actual items, most teachers would probably agree that they require some higher-level thinking on the part of students.

Teachers should not assume, however, that because such test items are possible to construct, that they themselves can construct them or that they would want to spend the time necessary to do so. These test items are designed by measure-ment experts, and are extensively field-tested to ensure that they are both valid and reliable. Neither of these conditions is available to most practicing educators, who have their next day's lessons to think about.

When teachers do try to design their own multiple-choice tests, they encounter three related, though somewhat distinct, difficulties:

♦ Ambiguity

A major challenge confronting test developers is to create multiple-choice test items in which the wrong answers are plausible but are unambiguously wrong. Ideally, these distracters (the wrong answers) should be incorrect in the same ways that student thinking is typically flawed, so that a student's pattern of wrong answers may reveal diagnostic information.

Such tests are very difficult to construct. Most teachers have had the experience of creating a test on which students can, by guessing or by using processes of elimination, determine the right answer even when they know very little about the subject.

♦ Authenticity

To engage students in meaningful work, it is helpful for assessment to be as authentic as possible. Students are more likely to produce work of good quality if the questions seem plausible and worthwhile. But to design an authentic multiple-choice test, one that elicits the desired knowledge and skill, is very difficult. Highly authentic questions tend to be long and cumbersome, while more focused questions are often found boring and unauthentic by students.

♦ Time

Good multiple-choice questions require a great deal of time to create and unless they are tested before being used, teachers cannot be sure that they are valid. That is, the question may be ambiguous or several of the choices may be plausible. Hence, students are justified in challenging such questions and evaluations based on them.

These factors, taken together, suggest that teachers attempting to create their own multiple-choice tests for complex learning are unlikely to be successful. Experts in test design can succeed more often than novices, but even experts are limited in what is possible through this technique.

INFLUENCE ON INSTRUCTION

Probably the most serious concern regarding the exclusive use of traditional testing relates to its effect on the instructional process. Because traditional tests are best suited to the assessment of low-level knowledge, such instructional goals are heavily represented (to the virtual exclusion of other, more complex, learning goals) in such tests.

It is well known that "what you test is what you get." Through our assessment methods we convey to students what is important to learn. When the tests we give reflect only factual or procedural knowledge, we signal to students that such knowledge is more important than their ability to reason, to solve problems, to work together collaboratively, or to write effectively. Because multiple-choice tests are best at evaluating students' command of factual knowledge, many students equate school learning with trivial pursuit, never realizing that their teachers value the expression of their own ideas, a creative approach to problems, or the design of an imaginative experiment.

The most powerful means teachers have at their disposal for shifting the culture of their classrooms to one of significant work is to change their assessment methodologies. While traditional tests have value, combining their use with alternative means sends an important signal to students regarding what sort of learning is valued in school. If good ideas and imaginative projects *count*, students will begin to shift their concept of the meaning of school.

SUMMARY

Traditional forms of assessment have many disadvantages. When they are used exclusively, they can undermine the best intentions of teachers. Traditional tests can evaluate only a narrow band of student learning and, even within that band, are extremely difficult to construct well.

THE BENEFITS OF PERFORMANCE ASSESSMENT

Many of the advantages of performance assessment are simply the reverse of the limitations of traditional testing. They enable teachers to assess students in all those aspects of learning that they value; in particular, writing and speaking, reasoning and problem-solving, psychomotor and social skills, and the entire affective domain. However, there are many other benefits to be derived as well. These are described in the following sections.

CLARITY OF CRITERIA AND STANDARDS

When teachers use performance assessment, they discover that they must be extremely clear, both to themselves and to their students, about the criteria that they will use to evaluate student work and about the standard of performance that they expect. For many teachers this clarity is greater than that required for traditional testing and requires that they give sustained thought to difficult questions, such as "What do I really want my students to be able to do?" and "What is most important in this unit?" and "How good is good enough?"

These questions, while some of the most important that teachers ever consider, tend to be obscured by the pressure of daily work and the normal routines of school life. The design of performance-assessment tasks puts them at the center. Most teachers find that although the questions are difficult to answer, their entire instructional program is greatly strengthened as a result of their effort.

PROFESSIONAL DIALOGUE ABOUT CRITERIA AND STANDARDS

If teachers create their performance assessments together, they must decide, together, how they will evaluate student work and what their standards will be. These are not easy discussions, but most teachers find them to be extremely valuable.

Occasionally, teachers find that one teacher's criteria for problem-solving, for example, are very different from another teacher's criteria. One teacher may believe that the process used is more important than whether the answer is correct. Another may believe the reverse. In designing a problem-solving task, if they are to evaluate student work together, they must resolve their differences. On the other hand, they could agree to disagree and each use his or her own procedure. But the conversation will have been valuable in isolating such a fundamental difference in approach.

IMPROVED STUDENT WORK

Virtually all teachers report improved quality of student work when performance assessment is used. This is due, no doubt, to several factors:

♦ Clarity of criteria and standards

Just as greater clarity as to criteria and standards is valuable to teachers and contributes to professional dialogue, it is essential for students. When students know what is expected, they are far more likely to be able to produce it than if they do not.

♦ Greater confidence in work

When students understand the criteria and standards to be used in evaluating their work, they can approach it with greater confidence. The criteria provide them with guidelines for their work, and they can estimate the time required to produce work of good quality. All this tends to increase student engagement and pride in their work.

♦ High expectations

When they make the standards for exemplary performance clear to students, teachers send an important signal about their expectations. They are saying to students, "Here is how I define excellence. Anyone here can produce work of such quality by applying sufficient effort." This is a powerful message for students; it brings excellence within their reach.

♦ Greater student engagement

When students are involved in performance tasks, particularly those that are highly authentic, they are more likely to be highly motivated in their work than if they are answering trivial pursuit-type questions. As a consequence of this engagement, the quality of student work is generally high.

IMPROVED COMMUNICATION WITH PARENTS

Student work produced as part of a performance assessment is extremely meaningful to parents. If collected in a portfolio and used for parent conferences, these products can serve to document student learning (or the lack of it). If necessary, a student's work may be shown to parents next to that of another (anonymous) student to illustrate differences in performance. Such documentation may be very helpful to teachers in persuading a parent of the need for additional educational services.

If student work as part of performance assessment is maintained in a portfolio, however, the selections should be made with care. There are many possible uses of a portfolio, and students can benefit from the reflection that accompanies their own selection of "best work" entries. But as a documentation of student progress, items should be chosen that reflect student performance in all the important instructional goals. For example, if a math program consists of 8 strands taught through 12 units, the selections made should document each of the units, and all of the strands. These issues are discussed more fully in Chapter 3.

SUMMARY

The use of performance assessment brings many important benefits beyond purely measurement issues to the culture of a classroom. These advantages result from clarity of criteria and standards, and they benefit teachers, students, and parents.

3

MAKING AN EVALUATION PLAN

Designing and implementing performance assessment entails a major investment of time and energy. To ensure that this investment is a wise one and that it yields the desired benefits, it is essential to work from a plan. How to develop such a plan and coordinate it with a school or district's curriculum, is the subject of this chapter.

A CURRICULUM MAP

A useful approach to developing an assessment plan for mathematics instruction is to begin with a consideration of goals in the mathematics curriculum as a whole. An assessment plan, after all, should have as its goal the assessment of student learning in the curriculum; it makes no sense in isolation from that curriculum. Therefore, a plan for assessment should be created with the whole curriculum in mind.

MAJOR OUTCOMES, GOALS, OR STRANDS

A good place to start in thinking about the assessment demands of the curriculum is to consider it's major outcomes, goals, or strands. Most listings of major mathematics outcomes, or the organization of mathematics goals by strand, are arranged, at least loosely, around the *Standards* published by the National Council of Teachers of Mathematics (NCTM) in 1989. These standards have had an enormous, and positive, influence on the teaching of mathematics, and have caused educators everywhere to think more deeply about what they teach and how to engage their students in conceptual understanding. The NCTM standards for grades K-4 are organized into eight major areas:

- Estimation
- Number sense and numeration
- Concepts of whole number operations and computation
- Geometry and spatial sense
- Measurement
- Statistics and probability
- Fractions and decimals*
- Patterns and relationships

(*Assessment of fractions and decimals is more appropriate for fourth grade and is not addressed in the tasks in this book.)

Four additional curriculum standards address the nature of mathematical thinking and focus on problem-solving, reasoning, communication, and making connections.

School mathematics has been taught as a fixed set of facts and procedures for computing numerical and symbolic expressions to find one correct answer. Current best practices are based on the beliefs that students should understand and reason with mathematical concepts, solve problems in diverse contexts, and develop a confidence in their own mathematical ability. Active environments, where academic concepts are taught in a context of real-life problems, are more beneficial to primary students.

When educators are planning an intellectually stimulating curriculum for primary students that is rich in content, they look to the *National Association for the Education of Young*

Children Position Paper on Developmentally Appropriate Practices. This document is a comprehensive summary of child development and learning recommendations for children from birth to eight years of age. The guiding principles are to:

- Teach to the "whole" child: physical, cognitive, social, and emotional
- Use an integrated curriculum approach
- Engage students in hands-on learning
- Present children with content that is relevant, engaging, and meaningful to them
- Provide small group projects that foster language interactions and dynamic discussions
- Promote positive peer interactions in a classroom community
- Assess what students know through authentic classroom observations and tasks

Primary teachers are aware of the stages of concept development with young children—exploration, inquiry, and utilization. Students actively explore all the possibilities in play. Then they are ready to participate in the introduction of numerical skill. The new learning takes on a totally new significance when students apply it to their own personal life. Students relate language to mathematical action and practice communicating in a precise dialogue.

Concepts are constructed over time and children encounter an idea several times before they can begin to form generalizations. For instance, the concept of pattern may be introduced to a kindergarten child as an exploration of an A-B-C pattern. First and second graders may discover growing or sequence patterns through an inquiry cycle. A visual model of numerical counting patterns may be utilized in second grade as a preparation for repeated addition and multiplication. Given multiple experiences, over time the child will generalize that pattern is a problem-solving tool.

Concepts can not always be assigned to a grade level because of the vast difference in previous experiences and the range of developmental stages in young children. It's not *when*, but *how* concepts are presented that allows all children access to understanding the big ideas in the mathematical curriculum. Teachers typically teach to a higher level than they assess with young children. Introduction to and experiences with the range of mathematical concepts are more critical in the early years than is complete mastery.

THE DEVELOPMENTAL STAGES OF MATHEMATICS

The *emerging mathematician* can recognize and identify numerals, use concrete and pictorial models to represent quantities and use manipulatives to count. This child is able to sort and collect data in concrete situations, identify tools that measure things, recognize some geometric shapes, and copy and build a simple pattern.

The *beginning mathematician* can order and compare numbers, use concrete and abstract models to represent quantities, and begin to understand the relationship between addition and subtraction. This child is able to recall some basic facts, make reasonable estimates, represent and record data, select tools to measure things, compare attributes of geometric figures, and name, extend, and build a more complex pattern.

The *developing mathematician* can relate counting groups of objects to place value concepts, use abstract models to represent quantities, and use a variety of approaches to compute. This child is able to recall basic facts, determine the reasonableness of an answer, generate, organize and analyze data, compare and select appropriate measuring tools, classify and sort two- and three-dimensional geometric shapes, and name, extend, and record complex patterns.

The *independent mathematician* can apply a well-developed understanding of mathematics to make connections in new situations, recall number combinations, solve problems using algorithms, and compute two- and three-digit problems with more than one operation. This child is able to reflect on and improve the thinking processes necessary to compute, analyze data, measure, combine geometric shapes, and apply patterns and relationships to new experiences.

These broad goals, outcomes, or strands provide the framework for curriculum planning They do not comprise a curriculum; that is developed from the outcomes for each grade level. But they do offer guidance for those preparing the curricula at each stage.

TOPICS OR UNITS

What students work on every day, and the way in which most mathematics textbooks are organized, is a series of topics or units, rather than outcomes or strands. For example, in a typical second grade mathematics text, the chapters concern:

♦ Addition expressions

♦ Subtraction expressions

♦ Place value

♦ Graphing and statistics

♦ Fractions

♦ Telling time

♦ Geometry

♦ Area and volume measurement

♦ Counting money

♦ Probability

Clearly, some of the topics fit well with some of the strands. For example, the concepts taught in the "geometry" chapter address the goals in the "geometry" strand. But some of the other connections are not nearly so obvious. In which chapter, for instance, is material related to "mathematics as communication" or "estimation" found? If educators are committed to addressing all the goals stated or implied in the NCTM *Standards*, or the equivalent document from their own state or district, then they must match the topics or units they teach with the goals inherent in those standards. The best technique to use for this purpose is a matrix, such as is described in the next section, and a sample of which is presented in Figure 3.1.

FIGURE 3.1. CURRICULUM/ASSESSMENT PLANNING MATRIX

Outcomes / Units or Topics	Number Operations	Functions & Algebra	Patterns & Relationships

Geometry & Measurement	Statistics & Probability	Problem Solving, Reasoning, & Communication	Skills & Tools

Creating the Curriculum Map

Across the top of the matrix are listed all the strands, major goals, or outcomes of the mathematics program. In the matrix provided, the ones listed are those developed by the NCTM. Down the left-hand side are listed all the topics or units in the year's curriculum, organized, insofar as can be known, in sequence. Then, for each unit or topic, teachers should consider which of the strands or outcomes the topic addresses, and place an X in the corresponding box.

In some cases, research is needed to know where to place the Xs. For example, if one of the major strands is estimation, many topics may be used to develop that skill, but some are probably better than others; estimation is probably better suited as a component of computation than of geometry. Furthermore, some textbooks will develop the skill of estimation in the context of one topic, others in another. It may be an empirical question, then, which topics may be used to develop which of the outcomes. This can be determined by examining the text in use.

What results from this process is a map of the curriculum, demonstrating the ways in which the different strands or outcomes are (or can be, given the textbook in use) addressed in each of the topics of the curriculum. No doubt some strands receive heavier emphasis than others. In most texts, for example, "computation" is much more heavily weighted than "patterns and functions."

The map may reveal large gaps in the curriculum. If, for example, the curriculum map shows that some of the outcomes are not adequately addressed by the program in use, then some adjustments must be made. It is possible, for instance, that a given curriculum lacks focus on an entire strand of the NCTM standards (as, for example, mathematical communication). In that case, educators have to determine in which topics they could develop that skill. Once determined, they can then add Xs to the appropriate boxes. For instance, they could decide to add, to each of their units, an objective (and the corresponding instructional activities) addressing the issue of student communication of the ideas of the unit, whether it is addition of fractions, or measurement. In that way, they would adequately address all the different *Standards*.

SUMMARY

A curriculum map can be used to define which units or topics in a curriculum may be used to help students acquire the knowledge and skills inherent in a state's mathematics framework. The map is created by local educators, using the appropriate framework and their own textbook, exercising professional judgment.

ASSESSMENT METHODOLOGIES

Once the curriculum map has been produced, educators must determine how each of the outcomes, and each of the topics, are to be assessed. Some will lend themselves to traditional testing; others will require more complex performance assessment.

THE ROLE OF TRADITIONAL TESTING

Many mathematics curriculum goals may be assessed through traditional testing. It is, and will always be, important for students to be able to perform accurate computations, to factor polynomials, and to execute a geometric proof. The correct use of algorithms is an important part of mathematical literacy. For all these reasons, educators would be ill-advised to abandon the use of traditional tests as part of their total assessment plan.

However, traditional testing is limited in what it can achieve. As teachers survey the curriculum map they have produced, they discover that some of the Xs they have written simply do not lend themselves to a multiple-choice or short-answer test. What kind of test, for example, could one construct that would assess students on the communication of ideas in statistics? Or on the use of patterns and functions to solve problems in geometry?

Moreover, many educators argue that the use of traditional tests, even in those areas of the curriculum where they seem to be best suited, can do actual harm because some students, and their teachers, confuse procedural knowledge with conceptual understanding. That is, students learn a procedure, an algorithm, for getting "the right answer" with little or no understanding of how or why the procedure works, of where it would be useful, or of what the algorithm accomplishes. Therefore, they can take a test and solve problems correctly, but with poor conceptual understanding. And if the assessment procedures used do not reveal that lack of understanding, the students may move along to more complex concepts, ones that build on the previous ones, with an increasingly shaky foundation.

Thus, while traditional tests may be highly useful in assessing certain aspects of the mathematics curriculum, they should be used with caution and with full awareness of their limitations.

THE PLACE FOR PERFORMANCE ASSESSMENT

Performance assessment is the technique of choice for evaluating student understanding of much of the mathematics curriculum. When students are asked to complete a task—when they are asked to explain their thinking—they reveal their understanding of complex topics.

Sometimes performance assessment in mathematics can consist of a small addition to traditional testing. For example, students might be asked to solve a fairly traditional problem, but then asked to explain why they selected the approach they did. Their explanation reveals their understanding of the process, or their lack of it, and serves to assess their skill in the communication of mathematical ideas.

In addition, the authentic application of mathematical procedures is highly motivational to students. Many students regard the applications problems (word problems) that they encounter in most mathematics textbooks with disbelief; their reaction is frequently one of "who cares?" With some thought, however, most teachers can create situations that students in their classes might actually encounter, which require the application of the mathematical ideas included in a given unit. The creation of such a task is the subject of Chapter 4, and the adaptation of an existing task is considered in Chapter 7.

A PLAN TO GET STARTED

The idea of creating (or even adapting) performance tasks for all those areas of the mathematics curriculum for which they would be well suited can be daunting. After all, if students as well as teachers are unfamiliar with such an approach, it is likely to take more time than planned. And because it is unfamiliar, everyone involved is likely to encounter unexpected difficulties. How, then, should one begin?

In general, one should start small. Once the techniques and practices of performance assessment are well understood, and once teachers and students both have some experience in the methodology, performance tasks may be used frequently, particularly if they are small ones. However, when beginning, it is recommended that teachers use performance tasks infrequently, at a rate, for example, of four to six per year. Such a schedule permits teachers the time to create or adapt their tasks to ensure that they accomplish their desired purposes and to evaluate student work carefully. If only one or two tasks are administered per quarter, they should be those that are likely to reveal the most information about student understanding.

Once teachers have acquired experience in the use of performance tasks, they may want to use them more frequently and more informally. However, even with experience, few teachers will administer more than two or three such tasks per month.

SUMMARY

Based on the curriculum map, educators can create an evaluation plan. This plan should include both traditional testing and performance assessment. As they move to performance assessment, teachers are advised to start small.

4

EVALUATING COMPLEX PERFORMANCE

The major advantage of multiple-choice or matching and true/false tests is the ease in scoring them; it does not take long to mark an answer right or wrong. Indeed, this speed and ease of correction is their primary value in large-scale testing programs; because standardized tests are machine scored and, consequently, inexpensive to administer, they can provide large amounts of data cheaply to school districts and states.

A student's performance on a multiple-choice or short-answer test may be described in terms of percentages. One student might score 87%; another 94%; still another 68%. But when teachers use other assessment methodologies, the concept of "percent correct" loses much of its meaning. What is 87% of an essay? How good (and good in what way) should a skit be to receive a score of 94%?

These are not simple questions, and their answers constitute the heart of performance assessment. But there *are* answers, and answers that respect the important measurement principles of equity, validity, and reliability. This chapter introduces the techniques of evaluating performance with a nonschool example and discussing each of the issues raised.

A NONSCHOOL EXAMPLE

All of the principles involved in the evaluation of complex performance may be illustrated by an everyday example—going to a restaurant. Reading through this example readers address, in a more familiar form, all of the issues that they encounter in designing systems of performance assessment for classroom use. Moreover, it becomes evident that the methods for evaluating performance reflect, at their heart, only common sense.

THE SITUATION

Imagine that we are opening a restaurant in your town and that we are now ready to hire waiters and waitresses. We know that it is important that the waiters and waitresses be skilled, so we want to hire the best that we can find. As part of our search, we have decided to eat in some existing restaurants to see if there are people working in these establishments that we can lure to our restaurant. Consequently, we are preparing to embark on our search mission.

THE CRITERIA

How will we know what to look for? We must determine the five or six most important qualities we would watch for in a good waiter or waitress. But because our focus is on "performance," we should list only those qualities that are visible to a customer (such as appearance), and not other qualities which, while they might be important to an employer (such as getting to work on time), are not seen by a customer.

A reasonable list of criteria includes such qualities as courtesy, appearance, responsiveness, knowledge, coordination, and accuracy. It is important to write the criteria using neutral, rather than positive, words. That is, for reasons that will become apparent shortly, we should write "appearance" rather than "neat."

These criteria could , of course, become a checklist. That is, we could eat in a restaurant and determine whether our server was courteous, or responsive, or knowledgeable, and so forth. We could answer each of the items with a "yes" or "no," and then count the "yeses." However, life tends to be more complex than a checklist—a waiter or waitress might be *somewhat* knowledgeable, *mostly* accurate, *a little bit* coordinated.

How do we accommodate these degrees of performance? How do we design a system that respects the complexity of the performance, yet that allows us to compare two or more individuals. The answer is to create a "rubric," a scoring guide.

THE SCORING GUIDE OR RUBRIC

Figure 4.1 is a rubric, which is simply a guide for evaluating performance.

FIGURE 4.1. WAITER/WAITRESS EVALUATION RUBRIC

	Level One	Level Two	Level Three	Level Four
Courtesy				
Appearance				
Responsiveness				
Knowledge				
Coordination				
Accuracy				

The criteria that are important for waiters and waitresses in our fledgling restaurant are listed in the left column. Across the top, are columns for different levels of performance. In this case, there are four levels. The double-line between levels two and three indicates that performance at levels three and four is acceptable, but performance at levels one and two is unacceptable. We could, then, broadly define the different levels as:

Level One: very poor; terrible; completely unacceptable

Level Two: not quite good enough; almost

Level Three: acceptable; good enough but not great

Level Four: wonderful; exemplary; terrific

In each box, then, we would write descriptions of actual performance that would represent each level for each criterion. For example, for "coordination" we might decide that an individual at Level One is someone who actually spilled an entire bowl of soup, or a cup of coffee, or who could not handle a tray of dishes; an individual at Level Two is someone who spilled a little coffee in the saucer, or who spilled some water while filling the glasses; a person at Level Three is someone who spilled nothing; and a person at Level Four is someone who balanced many items without mishap.

We could fill in the entire chart with such descriptions, and we would then be ready to go evaluate prospective employees. A possible profile might look like Figure 4.2:

FIGURE 4.2. A COMPLETED WAITER/WAITRESS RUBRIC

Name: Wendy Jones   **Restaurant: Hilltop Cafe**

	Level One	Level Two	Level Three	Level Four
Courtesy		X		
Appearance				X
Responsiveness			X	
Knowledge	X			
Coordination				X
Accuracy			X	

We still have to decide, of course, whether to hire this individual, or whether this individual was preferable to another candidate whose scores were all "3s." That is, we still have to determine how to arrive at a composite score for each individual so that we can compare them.

If we were using this approach for supervision rather than for hiring, we would not need to combine scores on the different criteria. We could use the scores for feedback and coaching. For example, because this individual is, apparently, not very knowledgeable, we could provide assistance in that area. We could then work on courtesy, and make sure that customers feel comfortable around this person. That is, for supervision purposes, the system is diagnostic and enables us to provide specific and substantive feedback on areas needing improvement.

SUMMARY

Creating a scoring rubric for a nonschool activity illustrates the principles involved in performance assessment.

MEASUREMENT AND PRACTICAL ISSUES

When we contemplate applying these principles to the evaluation of student performance, we encounter a number of issues which, while not technically complex, must be addressed before this approach can be implemented. It should be borne in mind that most teachers have rubrics in their minds for student performance; they apply these every time they grade a student's paper. However, communication is vastly improved if educators can be explicit about the criteria they use in evaluating student work and about what their expectations are. Achieving this clarity requires the teacher to address a number of technical and practical issues.

THE NUMBER AND TYPE OF CRITERIA

For a given performance, how many criteria should we have? For example, when evaluating a persuasive essay, how many different things should we look for? Should we evaluate organization separately from structure? What about the use of language; or specifically, the use of vocabulary; or correct spelling and mechanics? What about sentence structure and organization? Should we consider the essay's impact on us, the reader? Is it important that we be persuaded by the argument?

Clearly, some of these elements are related to one another: it would be difficult, in a persuasive essay, for example, to have good use of language independently of the vocabulary used. However, other criteria are completely separate from one another. A student's inadequacies in mechanics and spelling, for example, will not affect the persuasiveness of the argument, unless it is so poor as to hinder communication.

The number of criteria used should reflect, insofar as is possible, those aspects of performance that are simultaneously important and independent of one another. With primary students, three or four criteria that demonstrate organization and approach, mathematical accuracy, and oral or written presentations are appropriate. The criteria should reflect the age and skill of the students. With young children or special education students, for example, it might be necessary to identify specific aspects of punctuation that are evaluated—proper use of capital letters, commas, and semicolons—whereas for high school students these may all be clustered under "punctuation" and can include all aspects of mechanics.

However, when criteria are clustered in such a way that they include several elements, these should be specifically identified. Just as "appearance" in the waiter and waitress example might include the person's uniform, condition of the hair and nails, and general grooming, individual criteria should specify what elements are included. For example, "use of language" might include richness of vocabulary, use of persuasive words, and proper use of specialized terms.

Moreover, the criteria should reflect those aspects of performance that are truly most important, not merely those that are easiest to see or count. Thus, a rubric for writing should include more than spelling and mechanics; a rubric for problem-solving should include criteria dealing with the student's thought processes and methods of approach.

A rubric should not include so many criteria that it is difficult to use. On the other hand, it should include every important element. As a general rule, because most people cannot hold more than five or six items in their mind simultaneously, rubrics should not contain more than five or six criteria.

ANALYTIC VS. HOLISTIC RUBRICS

The waiter/waitress rubric developed in the previous section is an example of an *analytic* rubric, that is, different criteria are identified and levels of performance are described for each. A similar rubric, but with different criteria defined and described, is usable in the classroom to *analyze* the strengths and weaknesses of student work.

With a *holistic* rubric, on the other hand, the features of performance on all criteria for a given score are combined so that it is possible, for example, to describe a "Level Two" waiter, or a "Level Four" waitress. Such holistic judgments are necessary when a single score, such as on an advanced placement test, must be given. However, compromises are always necessary, because an individual piece of work usually does not include all the features of a certain level. Therefore, analytic rubrics are recommended for classroom use, because they provide much more complete information for feedback to students.

HOW MANY POINTS ON THE SCALE?

In the waiter/waitress example, we identified four points on the scale. That was an arbitrary decision; we could have selected more or less. Performance on any criterion, after all, falls along a continuum; designating points on a scale represents, to some degree, a compromise between practical demands and the complexity of real performance. However, in deciding on the number of points to use, there are several important considerations to remember:

♦ Fineness of distinctions

More points offer the opportunity to make very fine distinctions between levels of performance. However, scales with many points are time-consuming to use because the differences between the points are likely to be small.

♦ Even vs. odd

In general, an even number of points is preferable to an odd number. This relates to the measurement principle of central tendency, which states that many people, if given the opportunity, will assign a score in the middle of a range. If there is no middle, as on a scale with an even number of points, they are required to make a commitment to one side or the other.

However, these considerations apply to rubrics that are constructed for application to a single activity or type of performance. For *developmental* rubrics, a large number of points may be preferable. In a developmental rubric, students' performance over an extended period of time is monitored on a single rubric. Used most commonly in foreign language courses, such a rubric might define oral language proficiency from the most rudimentary level through the level displayed by a native speaker. Every student of the language performs somewhere, at all times, on that rubric, which might have, for example, 10 points. A second-year student might be functioning at, say, level three, while a fourth-year student might be at level five. Both would have made good progress, and yet have a distance to go before performing at the level of a native speaker. But for such purposes a developmental rubric with many points on the scale is extremely useful because it can be used to chart progress over many years.

DIVIDING LINE BETWEEN ACCEPTABLE AND UNACCEPTABLE PERFORMANCE

It is important to decide, at the outset, where the line will be between acceptable and unacceptable performance. This activity is at the heart of setting a standard because teachers thereby communicate, to their colleagues as well as to their students, the quality of work they expect.

In the waiter/waitress example, the line between acceptable and unacceptable performance was established between levels two and three. This, too, is arbitrary; it could just as well been put between levels one and two. When determining where to place the dividing line, educators should consider several points:

♦ Use

If a scoring rubric is to be used for formative evaluation, it is helpful to identify several levels of unacceptable performance so that teachers can know quickly whether a student's performance on a certain criterion is close to being acceptable, or is far away. Such knowledge can guide further instruction. On the other hand, if a rubric is to be used to make a summative judgment only, then it is less important whether a student's performance is close to the cut-off point; unacceptable is unacceptable, without regard to degrees of unacceptability.

♦ Number of points on the scale

If a scoring rubric is constructed with six, seven, or eight points, then the placement of the " unacceptable" line might be different than for a rubric with only four points. A five-point scale (while not ideal from the standpoint of having an odd number of points) allows two levels of unacceptable while also permitting finer degrees of excellence, with the upper levels representing, for example, barely acceptable, good, and excellent.

♦ Developmental vs. nondevelopmental rubrics

Clearly, for a developmental rubric that defines performance over an extended period of time, there is no need to define the distinction between acceptable and unacceptable performance in the same manner as for a performance-specific rubric. That is, it may be reasonable for a second-year language student to perform at level 3 on a 10-point scale, whereas such performance would not be good enough for a fourth-year student. In this case, judgments as to acceptability and expectations do not reside in the rubric, but in the use that is made of them in different settings.

TITLES FOR LEVELS OF PERFORMANCE

Closely related to the need to define the cut-off between acceptable and unacceptable performance is the requirement to broadly define the labels for each point on the rubric. Teachers often use words such as "unacceptable" and "exemplary." Although such descriptions might work even if students (or their parents) will see the rubric, such descriptions should be given some thought. Some educators prefer designations like "novice," "emerging," "proficient," and "distinguished." Decisions as to the best headings are matters for professional judgment and consensus.

DESCRIPTIONS OF PERFORMANCE

Descriptions for levels of performance should be written in language that is truly descriptive rather than comparative. For example, words such as "average" should be avoided, as in "the number of computational errors is average," and replaced by statements such as "the solution contains only minor computational errors." "Minor" will then have to be defined, as, for example, "an error not resulting in an erroneous conclusion," or "an error that was clearly based in carelessness."

GENERIC VS. TASK-SPECIFIC

Constructing a performance rubric for student work takes considerable time, particularly if it is a joint effort among many educators. The issue of time, and the desire to send a consistent signal to students and their parents regarding standards, are important reasons to try to create generic rubrics. Such rubrics may be used for many different specific tasks that students do.

The areas of student performance that appear to lend themselves best to generic rubrics are such things as lab reports, problem-solving, expository (or descriptive, or persuasive) essays, group projects, and oral presentations. Some of these, for example, oral presentations, are suitable for several different disciplines. It is highly valuable for students to know, in a consistent manner, that when they are preparing an oral presentation, it will always be evaluated, in every course, using the same criteria.

However, generic rubrics are not always possible, or even desirable. The elements of problem-solving, and certainly the levels of acceptable performance, are very different for high school sophomores than for second graders. Similarly, the specific elements of a lab report change as students become more sophisticated and more knowledgeable. So while there are many reasons to construct rubrics that are as generic as possible—intra- and cross-departmental discussions are highly recommended—it may not be possible to develop completely generic rubrics, even for those aspects of performance in which students are engaged over a period of many years. There are many types of tasks that require their own, task-specific rubric.

PROFESSIONAL CONSENSUS

When teachers work together to determine descriptions of levels of performance in a scoring rubric, they may find that they do not completely agree. This is natural and to be expected. After all, it is well-documented that teachers grade student work quite differently from one another.

Discussions about the proper wording for different levels of performance constitute rich professional experiences. While difficult, the discussions are generally enriching for everyone involved; most teachers find that their ideas can be enhanced by the contributions of their colleagues. Rubrics that are the product of many minds are generally superior to those created by individuals. In addition, if a number of teachers find that they can use the same, or similar, rubrics for evaluating student work, communication with students is that much more consistent, resulting in better quality work from students.

INTER-RATER AGREEMENT

Closely related to reaching consensus on the descriptions of performance levels is the matter of agreement on the rubric's application. The only way to be sure that there is agreement on the meaning of the descriptions of different levels is to apply the statements to samples of student work.

The importance of this issue cannot be emphasized enough. It is a fundamental principle of equity and fairness that evaluation of a student's work be the same regardless of who is doing the evaluating. However, teachers rarely agree completely at the beginning. Occasionally, two teachers will evaluate a single piece of student work very differently, even when they have agreed on the scoring rubric. In those cases, they generally discover that they were interpreting words in the rubric very differently, or that the words used were themselves ambiguous. Only by trying the rubric with actual student work are such difficulties revealed.

When preparing rubrics for evaluating student work, therefore, the project is not totally complete until examples of different levels of performance are selected to illustrate the points on the scale. Called "anchor papers" these samples serve to maintain consistency in scoring.

CLARITY OF DIRECTIONS

Another fundamental principle of fairness and equity concerns the directions given to students. Any criterion to be evaluated must be clearly asked for in the directions to a performance task. For example, if students are to be evaluated on their originality in making an oral presentation, something in the directions to them should recommend that they present it in an original or creative manner. Likewise, if students are to be evaluated on the organization of their data, they should know that organization is important. Otherwise, from a student's point of view, it is necessary to read the teacher's mind to guess what is important.

Some teachers even find that they can engage students in the development of the rubric itself. Students, they discover, know the indicators of a good oral presentation or of a well-solved problem. While students' thoughts are rarely well-enough organized to enable them to create a rubric on their own, their ideas make good additions to a teacher-drafted rubric.

There are many advantages to engaging students in the construction of a scoring rubric. Most obviously, they know what is included and can, therefore, focus their work. But even more importantly, students tend to do better work, with greater pride in it and with greater attention to its quality, when the evaluation criteria are clear. Suddenly, school is not a matter of "gotcha;" it is a place where excellent work is both defined and expected.

COMBINING SCORES ON CRITERIA

Occasionally, it is important to combine scores on different criteria and to arrive at a single evaluation. For example, teachers must occasionally rank students, or convert their judgments on performance to a grade or to a percentage. How can this be done?

In arriving at a single, holistic score, several issues must be addressed:

◆ Weight

Are all the criteria of equal importance? Unless one or another is designated as more or less important than the others, they should all be assumed to be of equal importance. Educators should have good reasons for their decisions as to weight, and these discussions can themselves constitute important professional conversations. As an example, when creating the waiter/waitress rubric, we could have determined that "knowledge" is the most important criterion and that it is worth twice the value of the others. Then, our rubric, and the points possible from each point, would appear as shown in Figure 4.3.

◆ Calculations

How should the scores be calculated? Clearly, the easiest technique is to convert the assigned scores on each criterion, as reflected in the weights assigned to each criterion, to a percentage of the total possible number of points, using a formula similar to this:

FIGURE 4.3. WEIGHTED WAITER/WAITRESS RUBRIC

Name: __Wendy Jones__   Restaurant: __Hilltop Cafe__

	Level One	Level Two	Level Three	Level Four
Courtesy Weight = 1		X		
Appearance Weight = 1				X
Responsiveness Weight = 1			X	
Knowledge Weight = 2	X			
Coordination Weight = 1				X
Accuracy Weight = 1			X	

Score Assigned x Weight = Criterion Score
Criterion Score on Each Criterion = Total Score
Total Score / Total Possible Scores = Percentage Score

Using this procedure for Wendy Jones, her point score is:

Courtesy: 2 (2 x 1)
Appearance: 4 (4 x 1)
Responsiveness: 3 (3 x 1)
Knowledge: 2 (1 x 2)
Coordination: 4 (4 x 1)
Accuracy: 3 (3 x 1)

Total: 18

On this rubric, the maximum possible score for each criterion is:

Courtesy: 4
Appearance: 4

Responsiveness:	4
Knowledge:	8
Responsiveness:	4
Accuracy:	4
Total:	28

Thus, in our example, Wendy Jones received a score of 18 which, when divided by 28, is 64%.

- Cut score

  What is the overall level of acceptable performance? We defined earlier the line between acceptable and unacceptable performance for each criterion. However, we must now determine a score which, overall, represents acceptable performance. We could set it as a percentage, for example 70%, in which case Wendy Jones would not be hired in our restaurant. Alternatively, we could establish a rule that no more than one criterion may be rated below three. This decision, like all the others made in constructing a performance rubric, is a matter of professional judgment.

TIME

Not only for large-scale assessment, but also in the classroom, teachers know that multiple choice, short-answer, matching, and true/false tests take far less time to score than essay or open-ended tests. It is a relatively simple matter to take a stack of student tests and grade them against an answer key. Many educators fear that using performance tasks and rubrics will consume more time than they have or want to devote to it.

There is some validity to this concern. It is true that the evaluation of student work, using a rubric, takes more time than does grading student tests against a key. And the rubric itself can take considerable time to create.

However, there are two important issues to consider. One relates to the increasing ease of using performance tasks, and the second relates to the benefits derived from their use.

♦ Decreasing time demands

When they are just beginning to use performance tasks and rubrics, many teachers find that the time requirements are far greater than those needed for traditional tests. However, as they become more skilled, and as the rubrics they have developed prove to be useful for other assignments or other types of work, teachers discover that they can evaluate student work very efficiently and, in many cases, in very little more time, if any, than that required for traditional tests.

♦ Other benefits

Most teachers discover that the benefits derived from increased use of performance tasks and rubrics vastly outweigh the additional time needed. They discover that students produce better quality work and that students take greater pride in that work. When performance tasks and rubrics are used as a component in assigning grades, teachers find that they can justify their decisions far more reliably than before they used rubrics.

SUBJECTIVITY VS. OBJECTIVITY

An important reservation about the use of rubrics to evaluate student work concerns their perceived "subjectivity" when compared to the "objectivity"of multiple-choice tests. Such fears, while understandable, are unjustified.

First, it is important to remember that the only objective feature to a multiple-choice test is its scoring; answers are unambiguously right or wrong. However, many professional judgments have entered into making the test itself, and even into determining which of the possible answers is the correct one. Someone must decide what questions to ask and how to structure the problems. These decisions reflect a vision of what are the important knowledge and skill for students to demonstrate, and are based on professional judgment.

Similarly, in the construction of a scoring rubric, many decisions must be made. These, too, are made on the basis of professional judgment. But the fact that they are made by teachers in their classrooms, rather than by testing companies, does not make them less valid judgments. It may be argued that, if well thought out, such judgments are superior to those màde by anonymous agencies far from the realities of one's own classroom.

In any event, both scoring rubrics to evaluate student work and standardized tests are grounded in professional judgment. They are absolutely equivalent on that score. In both cases, it is the quality of the judgments that is important, and the classroom-based judgment may be as good as that made by the testing company.

SUMMARY

In using scoring rubrics to evaluate student work, many issues must be considered. However, these issues, such as the number of points on the scale or the importance of inter-rater agreement, are primarily matters of common sense.

5

CREATING A
PERFORMANCE
TASK

The evaluation plan that results from the analysis of curriculum outcomes and topics (see Chapter 3) provides the guidelines needed to actually design performance tasks. As part of that plan, educators will have decided which topics or units lend themselves to which broader outcome goals or strands, and will have determined the best evaluation strategy for each. This analysis provides the basis for developing specifications (or requirements) for each performance task.

It is important to remember that a performance task is not simply something fun to do with one's students; it is not just an activity. While it may involve student activity, and it may be fun, it is highly purposeful. A performance task is intended to assess learning, and it must be designed with that fundamental purpose in mind. In the design of performance tasks, a number of factors must be considered. These are described in this chapter.

SIZE OF PERFORMANCE TASKS

Performance tasks may be large or small. Large tasks take on many of the characteristics of instructional units, and students tend to derive many benefits from them in addition to those related to assessment. Large tasks may require a week or more to complete; they are typically complex and authentic, and require students to synthesize information from many sources. Small tasks, on the other hand, are more like open-ended test questions in which students solve a problem, for example, and then explain their reasoning. Usually, they may be completed in a single class period or less. Naturally, tasks may also be of medium length and complexity.

Primary students may be more successful with smaller tasks that allow them to reach a target performance or learn a new skill. Chunking larger tasks—breaking them into smaller tasks with simplified directions—can be used for presenting new content. Keep in mind that younger students may not be independent readers and may need the directions repeated orally, over the course of the task.

In deciding whether to use performance tasks that are large or small, educators must consider a number of factors.

PURPOSE

Teachers should be very clear about their purpose in using the performance task. What do they hope and plan to derive from it? Are their purposes purely those of assessment, or do they hope to accomplish some instructional purposes as well?

♦ Small tasks are primarily suitable for purely assessment purposes

If a teacher has taught a concept, for example, the distinction between area and perimeter, and simply wants to know that students understood that concept, then a small performance task is desirable. Such a task will ask students to solve a relatively small problem, to explain their thinking, and to show their work. However, it will not, in itself, also contain activities to be completed as part of the task. The task itself is designed purely for assessment.

◆ Large tasks carry instructional purposes as well as assessment ones

Occasionally, a teacher will want students to also learn new content as a result of completing an assessment task. If so, a larger task, spread over a number of days, involving many subactivities, will accomplish the purposes better than a small task.

◆ Large tasks are better suited to culminating assessments than are small ones

If performance tasks are to be used as culminating assessments, they are better if they are quite large and if they tap a number of different types of skills. However, if performance tasks are to be used for assessing a small part of the curriculum, small tasks are more useful, because they can be administered frequently and because the results can be used for adjusting instruction.

The purpose of the assessment is a major factor, then, in determining whether performance tasks should be large or small.

CURRICULUM PRESSURE AND TIME DEMANDS

Generally speaking, when teachers are under pressure to cover many topics in the curriculum, and consequently have little time to spend on any one topic, they may find that small performance tasks are all that they have time to use. Large tasks, while they include many benefits not derived from small ones, do require lots of time, frequently more than many teachers have to devote to them.

SKILL IN GETTING STARTED

Most educators, when they are just beginning to use performance tasks, are unsure of what they are doing. In such situations, it is a good idea to use the "start small" principle.

When the teacher is not sure whether the directions to students are clear on a task, for example, it is better to discover whether they are clear after the students have spent a class period, rather than a week, completing the task. Less time has been lost, and there may well be an opportunity to attempt another version of the task, or a different task, later.

SUMMARY

The size of a performance task is best determined by its purpose (immediate or culminating assessment, or instruction) and by the time constraints and experience of the teacher. In general, it is recommended that teachers begin their efforts with performance assessment using tasks that are small rather than large. This provides the opportunity to experiment with a new methodology in a way that carries low stakes for success, for both the students and the teacher.

The tasks in this book were expressly selected to apply at many different skill levels by modifying the range of numbers. For instance, kindergarten students may be using numbers 1 to 10, first graders may be working with numbers up to 50, second graders with numbers up to 100, and third graders up to 1,000. Tasks can also be varied for each grade level by increasing or decreasing the amount of scaffolding provided by the teacher or other peers.

CRITERIA FOR GOOD PERFORMANCE TASKS

There is no doubt that some performance tasks are better than others. What makes the good ones good? How can teachers, in designing or selecting performance tasks, ensure that they are the best possible tasks? Several important qualities of good performance tasks are described in the following material.

ENGAGING

The single most important criterion of performance tasks is that they are engaging to students; it is essential that they be of interest and that students want to put forth their best effort. This suggests that the questions asked should have intrinsic merit—that students don't read the question and respond "So what?" or "Who cares?"

How does one find or create engaging tasks? As with so much else in education, professional judgment is the key. Successful instructional activities can be a good place to begin. Most teachers know which activities or which types of activities are successful with their students. One of these activities, when adapted to the demands of assessment, might make a good performance task. When reviewing tasks that others have created, one important criterion to always bear in mind is whether the task is likely to be engaging to students.

AUTHENTICITY

Related to engagement is the issue of authenticity. Students tend to be more interested in those situations that resemble real life rather than in those that are completely divorced from any practical application. In addition, performance tasks that reflect the messiness of real life make demands on students that more sanitized situations do not. Other things being equal, it is preferable to design or adapt performance tasks that represent authentic applications of knowledge and skill. Such authenticity requires students to use their knowledge and skill in much the same way it is used by adult practitioners in that field. A template to be used for designing authentic tasks is provided as Figure 5.1.

However, authenticity is not always possible. Some important school learning is purely abstract, or makes sense only within its own context. For example, when we want students to demonstrate that they can analyze a character in literature, we must ask them to do that, even though such a task has no exact equivalents in real life. A student's skill in analyzing a literary character assesses not only how well the student understands the character, but the degree to which the student understands the structure of the piece of literature of which the character is a part.

Similarly, much of mathematics is highly formal and abstract. Although teachers care that students can apply their mathematical knowledge to practical situations, there is much of mathematics, such as number theory, which is internal to the discipline. Such knowledge must be assessed, and a

FIGURE 5.1. PERFORMANCE TASK DESIGN WORKSHEET

Designers _____

_____

School/District _____ Grade _____

Course _____ Topic _____

Outcome(s) _____

_____

Task Title

Brief description of the task (what students must do and what product will result):

Directions to the students:

Criteria to be used to evaluate student responses:

constructed-response question is preferable to a multiple-choice item. However, such a question will probably not reflect authentic application.

ELICITS DESIRED KNOWLEDGE AND SKILL

A good performance task must assess what we want it to assess. It must, in other words, be aligned to the instructional goals that we are interested in measuring. Furthermore, the task should be designed in such a way that a student can complete the task correctly *only* by using the knowledge and skills being assessed.

We should never underestimate our students in this regard. Although most students are not devious, most try to complete a task with as little risk and/or effort as possible. If they see a way to do the task, even by short-circuiting our intentions, they may well do it that way. Teachers should, therefore, create tasks that are as tight as possible, without being unduly rigid.

ENABLES ASSESSMENT OF INDIVIDUALS

Many performance tasks that sound imaginative are designed to be completed by students working in groups. Although such tasks may be valuable instructional activities and are certainly fun for the students, they cannot be used for the assessment of individuals. Assessment, after all, concerns the evaluation of *individual* learning; a performance task in which the contributions of different individuals is obscured cannot be used for such evaluation.

It is possible, of course, to design a performance task that includes both group and individual elements. For example, a group of students may be given some data and asked to analyze it. However, if the analysis is done as a group, each student should be required to produce an independent summary of what the data shows, and each individual's paper should be evaluated independently.

Even in such a situation, however, the information for the teacher is somewhat compromised. When reading the work of an individual, a teacher knows only what that student could produce *after having participated in a group with other students*. With a different group of peers, that same student might have demonstrated much greater, or far less, understanding.

In general, then, it is preferable to create individual performance tasks if these are to be used solely for assessment purposes. If the goal also includes instructional purposes, then compromises on the individuality of the assessment tasks may be necessary.

CONTAINS CLEAR DIRECTIONS FOR STUDENTS

Any good performance task includes directions for students that are both complete and unambiguous. This is a fundamental principle of equity and good measurement. Students should never be in doubt about what it is they are to do on a performance task; the directions should be clear and complete. That does not mean that the directions should be lengthy; on the contrary, shorter directions are preferable to lengthier ones.

The directions should specifically ask students to do, whatever it is that on which they will be evaluated. For example, if one of the assessment criteria for a mathematics problem involves the organization of information, students should be specifically instructed to present their information in an organized manner.

Related to the question of directions is that of *scaffolding*, that is, how much support should students receive in accomplishing the performance task? In a mathematics problem that involves a multistep solution, for example, should the students be prompted for each step or is that part of the problem? The answer to this question relates to the purposes of the assessment, and to the age and skill level of the students. In general, of course, less scaffolding is more authentic than more scaffolding; most problems are not presented to us with an outline of how to solve them. In general, then, it is preferable to provide students with problems without scaffolding that represent the optimal challenge for them to determine the proper approach on their own. An intermediate position is to present the problem without scaffolding, and to then offer tips for the students to consider if desired. These tips can contain suggestions that, if followed, provide guidance for a possible approach to the problem.

SUMMARY

Good performance tasks share a number of important criteria. These should be borne in mind as tasks are designed.

THE DESIGN PROCESS

Now that the criteria for a performance task are clearly in mind, it is time to create one. What process should be followed? While there are several possible approaches, an effective one is described in the following material.

CREATE AN INITIAL DESIGN

With the specifications and criteria in mind, create an initial draft of a performance task to assess a given combination of student understanding and skill. This task may be created using the format provided in Figure 5.2, on the next page, and may, if authenticity is desired, follow the template offered in Figure 5.1 on p. 56. This initial draft should be considered as just that, an initial draft; it will almost certainly be revised later in the process.

OBTAIN COLLEAGUE REVIEW

Persuade one or more colleagues to review your work. These may be teachers who work in the same discipline as you, or with the same age students, or teachers with very different responsibilities. Each approach has its advantages and its drawbacks.

Teachers with different responsibilities are more likely to catch ambiguity or lack of clarity in the directions to students than are teachers who are as expert in the field as you. On the other hand, expert colleagues are better able to spot situations in which the task is not completely valid; that is, situations in which students would be able to complete the task successfully without the desired knowledge and skill. Therefore, a colleague review that includes a combination of content experts and nonexperts is ideal.

PILOT TASK WITH STUDENTS

Not until a performance task is tried with students is it possible to know whether it can accomplish its desired purpose. Only then can teachers know whether the directions are clear, whether all elements are properly requested, and whether the task truly elicits the desired knowledge and skill.

FIGURE 5.2. PERFORMANCE TASK DESIGN

Authentic Simulation

Outcome: _____

Topic: _____

You are (student or adult role or profession)

Who has been asked by (audience or superior)

To (accomplish a specific task)

Using (resources)

Under the constraints of (as found in such a situation)

Your work will be judged according to (criteria)
(Attach a rubric)

Based on Worksheets from the High Success Network and CLASS

Piloting with students is also the only way to know the degree to which the task is engaging to them.

Students are likely to be extremely honest in their reaction to a performance task. While it is possible to collect their feedback formally, it is generally evident from their level of engagement and from the quality of their responses whether the task is a good one or not.

REVISE PERFORMANCE TASK

As a result of the colleague review and the pilot with students, the draft task will probably require some revision. This revision might be a major rewrite or a reconceptualization of the entire task. More likely, it will be only a minor revision—to make the task clearer, or less cumbersome, or to slant it differently.

Once revised, the task is ready for the formal process of rubric design discussed in Chapter 6. However, teachers should be aware that the task may need further revision after the scoring rubric is written; that exercise frequently reveals inadequacies (usually minor) in the task itself.

SUMMARY

The process of task design has several steps, all of which should be completed. A performance task should not be used for actual assessment until it has been piloted with students. This suggests that at least a year will elapse between the decision to embark on a program of performance assessment and the implementation of such a system.

6

CREATING A RUBRIC

To use a performance task to evaluate student learning, a guide for evaluating student work (in other words, a rubric) is needed. The development of the task and the application of the rubric should be considered an iterative process (as each is developed and used, it suggests changes in the other) with the final combination of task and rubric evolving over time. This chapter includes guidance for the design of a rubric for a task.

DRAFTING A SCORING RUBRIC

Generally speaking, the criteria to be used in evaluating student work will have been identified in the course of developing a performance task. However, to convert these criteria into an actual scoring rubric, they must be elaborated and further defined. Although holistic rubrics have their uses (for example, in the summative evaluation of student work for awarding a diploma), this section focuses on the design of analytic rubrics. Figure 6.1 provides a general format for developing a rubric.

FIGURE 6.1. PERFORMANCE RUBRIC

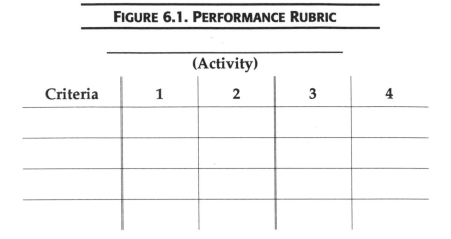

Criteria	(Activity)			
	1	2	3	4

Copyright 1996, Princeton Education Associates. All Rights Reserved. Reproduced by permission.

GENERIC OR TASK-SPECIFIC?

The first question to be asked and answered concerns the degree of task specificity of the rubric. If, for example, the rubric is being developed for a group mathematics project, could the same rubric be used for other projects, or is its use confined to this particular one? Indeed, could elements of the rubric, for example the elements concerned with making a group presentation, be used for other disciplines as well? Are there enough similarities between group presentations for mathematics, science, and social studies, for instance, that the same evaluation guide could be used for all of them?

In a sense, generic rubrics are more useful than task-specific ones. Creating rubrics is time-consuming, and the more broadly they may be applied, the more useful and powerful they are. However, sometimes a common rubric will have to be adapted for use in other situations and in other disciplines; while many of the elements are the same, the ways in which they appear in student work are sufficiently different to warrant independent consideration.

TASK, GENRE-SPECIFIC, OR DEVELOPMENTAL?

Another important question to be considered when creating a rubric is whether the rubric will be used on a single task (or a single type of task) or whether it will be used developmentally with students as they progress through many years of school. That is, will the rubric under development for a mathematics project, for example, be applied only to this particular project, which students do in the third grade, or could it also be used with students throughout the district, including those in high school as well as in elementary school?

If the rubric is to be used developmentally, it will probably have many more points on it, and the criteria may be written differently, than if the rubric is to be used for a single task. A developmental rubric is useful for a school in which students have mathematics portfolios, and may be helpful in charting progress over time. However, a developmental rubric may not be as useful for any particular task as one created specifically for that task.

DETERMINING CRITERIA

Once the question of task-specificity or developmental rubric has been answered, the next most important step in creating a scoring rubric is to identify the criteria to be evaluated. The importance of attending carefully to this step cannot be overstated. It is in the determination of criteria that educators define important aspects of performance, and define, for both themselves and their students, what they mean by good quality. When defining criteria, several issues should be considered:

◆ Type of criteria

In mathematics, an essential criterion almost always concerns mathematical accuracy. Is the answer correct? Are computational errors major or minor? Are answers correctly labeled? Are all possible answers found?

But in addition to computational accuracy, what else is important? What about conceptual understanding? Do students reveal, either through their approach to the problem or through the errors they make, that they have no understanding of the underlying concepts? Does the problem require a plan? If so, have students organized their information? Have they approached the problem in a systematic manner? Is the work presented neatly? Can a reader follow the student's line of reasoning?

In addition, a mathematics project might require that students collaborate with each other. How successfully do they do this? Do they establish a good division of labor, or do one or two students dominate the group? If the students make a presentation as part of the project, do they explain their thinking clearly? Are the other students interested in the presentation? Can they follow it? Is it engaging? It is important that the criteria identified for a task not consist only of those that are easiest to see (such as computational accuracy). The criteria should, taken together, define *all* the aspects of exemplary performance, even if some of them are somewhat challenging to specify and to evaluate.

One successful approach to the identification of criteria is to consider the task, and to imagine an excellent student response to it. What would such a response include? The answer to that question can serve to identify important criteria. Alternatively, many teachers do the task themselves prior to assigning it to their students, creating, in effect, an exemplary response, and appreciating the issues inherent in the task for students.

♦ Number and detail of criteria

There is no single best answer to the question "how many criteria?" Clearly, all important aspects of performance should be captured in the criteria. Moreover, those aspects of performance that are independent of one another should be designated as separate criteria.

It is possible to designate too many criteria, and for them to be too detailed. The resulting rubric is then cumbersome and time-consuming to use. On the other hand, a rubric that is too economical may not provide adequate information to help students improve their performance. The number and level of detail of the rubric, then, is partly a matter of how it is to be used, and partly of the age and skill level of the students. Rubrics used with special needs students, for example, are often made in great detail, so both teachers and students know where improvement efforts should be focused.

♦ Subcriteria or elements

Sometimes several criteria are related to one another, or one may be considered a subcategory of another. In that case, the criteria may contain subcriteria or elements within them. For example, if students make a presentation as part of the mathematics project, the overall criterion might be "quality of presentation" with subcriteria of "clarity," "originality and energy," and "involvement of all group members."

Occasionally, when educators think critically about the qualities they would look for in good student performance, they recognize that the task, as written, does not elicit those qualities. That is, students could do the task and not demonstrate the defined criteria. In that case, the directions must be rewritten, or the task restructured, to elicit the desired performance.

NUMBER OF POINTS

The question of the number of points on a scoring scale is closely related, of course, to whether the rubric is task-specific or developmental. If developmental, it will almost certainly have more points than if it is task-specific. And if it is developmental, the number of points should reflect the age range over which the rubric will be applied. For skills such as problem-solving or graphing that develop from kindergarten through 12th grade, a scale with 10 points would be reasonable.

But even for task-specific rubrics, educators must decide on the number of points. As explained previously, an even number is preferable to an odd number, because it prevents the phenomenon known as central tendency. But beyond that, there are several considerations to keep in mind.

♦ Detail in distinctions

With a larger number of points on a scale, fine distinctions are required when evaluating student work. While such detail can provide finely tuned feedback to students, a rubric with many points is cumbersome and time-consuming to use. For practical purposes, a rubric with four to six points is recommended. The ones in this collection all contain four points.

♦ Dividing line between acceptable and unacceptable performance

It is helpful, at the outset, to determine the dividing line between acceptable and unacceptable performance. On a four-point scale, this line is either between one and two or between two and three. That placement is determined by where the greater detail is the more useful; that is, is it more useful to be able to specify degrees of inadequacy, or degrees of adequacy?

♦ General headings for different points

The different points on the scale may be called simply by their numbers. On a 4-point scale, then, they would be 0, 1, 2, and 3 or 1, 2, 3, and 4. Alternatively, they could be 10, 20, 30, and 40. Alternatively, the points can be given names, such as "novice," "proficient," "exemplary," "great!" If this approach is taken, use positive, supportive words (such as "emerging") rather than negative ones (such as "inadequate.)

DESCRIPTIONS OF LEVELS OF PERFORMANCE

Once the criteria and the number of scale points have been determined, it is time to actually write the descriptions of levels of performance. Again, this step is critical, and includes a number of factors.

♦ The language used

The words used to specify the qualities of different levels of performance should be descriptive, rather than comparative. For example, words such as "average" should be avoided. The descriptions of levels of performance serve to further define the criteria, and are further defined themselves only when accompanied by actual samples of student work, called anchor papers.

♦ All subcriteria or elements defined

If the criteria contain subcriteria, each of these elements should be described in each of the performance descriptions. For example, if a criterion on presentation includes accuracy, originality, and involvement of all group members, then the descriptions for each of the levels should describe the group's presentation with respect to all those elements.

♦ Distance between points

To the extent possible, the distance between the points on a scale should be equal. That is, the distance between a three and a four should not be much greater than the distance between a two and a three.

♦ The line between acceptable and unacceptable performance

Where the line between acceptable and unaccept-able performance is established should receive particular scrutiny. While the highest and lowest levels of performance are the easiest to describe, those in the middle, those that define acceptable and unacceptable performance, are the most im-portant. It is here, after all, that educators define their standards and specify the quality of work on which they insist and of which they expect mas-tery. It is recommended that these levels be de-scribed with particular care.

SUMMARY

The most critical step in the development of a scoring ru-bric for evaluating student performance is its initial design. For this process, a number of factors—such as whether it is generic or specific, the actual criteria, the number of points on the scale, and the language used to define the points—must be considered.

PILOTING THE RUBRIC WITH STUDENT WORK

The proof of a rubric is in its use with student work. Not until a rubric is used to evaluate actual student work will its authors know whether it is viable. Several steps are recom-mended.

EVALUATING A SAMPLE OF STUDENT WORK

A good place to begin is to collect a small number (about 10) of samples of student work that represents the full range of probable responses in the class. The sample should include those students from whom the best work is expected, as well as those whose work might not be adequate. If possible, the pieces of work should be anonymous; they could be num-bered and referred to by their numbers.

Then, with the rubric in hand, evaluate the student work using the draft rubric. The form in Figure 6.2 may be used, with the criteria listed (or numbered) down the side, and the levels of performance for different students specified in the column corresponding to each one. Surveying the entire page, then, provides a summary of the levels of performance represented by the class as a whole, and can offer guidance as to the next instructional steps that may be needed.

FIGURE 6.2. PERFORMANCE ASSESSMENT

Evaluation Results

Evaluator _____ Date _____

Task _____ Grade Level _____

Student / Criteria	1	2	3	4	5	6	7	8

INTER-RATER AGREEMENT

It is possible, however, that the rubric or its use is not yet reliable. The only way to check this is to request assistance from a colleague. It is recommended that another educator be introduced to the task and the rubric, and be provided with the same sample of student work initially used. This person should then evaluate the same students and assign scores on each criterion based on the draft rubric.

Scores for each student on each criterion should then be compared. Clearly, the goal is for all scores to be the same, although this is unlikely to occur. Any discrepancies should then be discussed until the cause of the discrepancy is understood. Most frequently, discrepancies are caused by a lack of clarity in the words used in the performance levels.

REVISING THE RUBRIC AND/OR THE TASK

As a result of evaluating student work and of comparing scores assigned with those of another educator, it is likely that the rubric (and possibly also the task) will require some revision. With luck, these revisions will not be extensive and will serve to clarify points of ambiguity.

LOCATING ANCHOR PAPERS

As a final step in rubric design, samples of student work that represent different points on the scale for each of the different criteria should be identified. By keeping these from year to year, it is possible to chart the course of general improvement in student work over time. In addition, only through the use of anchor papers can educators be sure that their standards are remaining the same and are not gradually drifting.

SUMMARY

Not until a scoring rubric has been piloted with actual student papers will its designers know whether it is effective.

7

ADAPTING EXISTING PERFORMANCE TASKS AND RUBRICS

Educators can often save time and effort by adapting an existing task, with its scoring rubric, to their own use. Using this approach, they benefit from the work of others and still have a task that reflects their own unique needs.

There are many sources of performance tasks that can be adapted, in addition to those in this book. Many textbook publishers now offer some performance tasks and rubrics as part of their package. Some state departments of education have also created prototype tasks and the National Council of Teachers of Mathematics (NCTM) has published some examples. The techniques for adapting existing tasks are described in this section.

MATCHING OUTCOMES, TOPICS, AND STUDENTS

The first step in identifying tasks suitable for adaptation is to match the outcomes and topics assessed by the task with those in one's own curriculum. The performance tasks in this book have been aligned with the strands in the NCTM *Standards,* and with different topics found in most mathematics curricula. By examining those alignments, educators can determine whether a given task is of value to them in assessing student mastery of their own curriculum.

It is unlikely that such a match will be perfect. First, a performance task may ask students to perform an operation or complete an activity that students in a given class have not yet learned. Alternatively, a scoring rubric sometimes includes criteria that do not reflect a district's curriculum. In those cases, either the task or the rubric has to be adjusted.

Second, a particular task may have been developed for students who are very different from those in one's own class. For a task to be effective, it must be one to which students can relate.

SUMMARY

To determine whether a performance task can be used as written, educators must match the task's outcomes and topics with those in their own curriculum, and must also consider the abilities of their own students.

ADJUSTING THE TASK

The actual task may need adaptation, either to reflect a school's curriculum, to make it more meaningful and relevant to the students concerned, or to adjust the situation to local conditions. Each of these reasons should be considered separately,

TO REFLECT A SCHOOL'S CURRICULUM

If there is poor alignment between a performance task and a school's curriculum, the task must be adjusted to correct it. Such an adjustment will take the form of adding to, subtracting from, or simply changing the requirements for the students. For example, a particular task might require students to find the average of a group of numbers as one step in solving a problem. If students in a particular class have not yet learned how to do that, the task should be adjusted to eliminate that step.

Alternatively, one school's curriculum might teach estimation in the course of doing work in measurement, while a performance task involving measurement does not, as written, ask the students to estimate their answer before measuring and calculating. In that case, adapting the task might involve adding a step requiring the students to estimate.

TO REFLECT A GROUP OF STUDENTS

Sometimes a task is designed with the characteristics of a particular group of students in mind and it is not ideally suited to others. Different classes of students are not identical in the sophistication of their thinking, and in the knowledge and skills that they bring to a class. Therefore, a performance task that is to be used with any group of students must be considered with the characteristics of that group in mind.

This factor is often reflected in the amount of scaffolding provided to students as they solve problems. For lower-functioning students, a task might have to be written with more "tips" for solution than are needed for more advanced students. Alternatively, a single task might be broken into several subtasks that students work on separately.

On the other hand, a task can be made more difficult and complex. A task that asks students simply to find an answer can be adjusted to also require an explanation of why a certain approach was employed. Or, a task that includes many suggestions about how students should proceed could be rewritten with just the question and fewer or no "tips" to the student. Each of these efforts will make the task more challenging, and may make it suitable for a more advanced group of students.

If a performance task is adjusted to reflect a group of students, particularly if it is deliberately made more or less challenging, it should be adapted purposefully, with the changes noted when student progress is monitored. If, for example, a task is deliberately simplified for a group of students, it should be clear to any reader of those students' records that the curriculum outcomes on which they were evaluated were different from those of another group of students.

TO ENHANCE ITS RELEVANCE

Another type of adaptation that might be warranted is that which makes a performance task more suitable to a local situation and, therefore, more relevant and meaningful to a group of students. For example, a task might ask students to calculate the amount of money they could earn by recycling their household cans, bottles, and plastic containers. If, however, steel cans and plastic cannot be recycled in a particular area, revise the task so that it concerns only aluminum cans and glass bottles.

Alternatively, an entire situation might be changed to reflect local conditions. For instance, a performance task might concern calculating the floor area of a school's classrooms for the purpose of recommending the purchase of carpeting. If, however, the school is about to have all its walls painted, the students could make those calculations instead, and actually make a presentation of their findings to the school district's maintenance department. Efforts to enhance relevance and authenticity pay big dividends in enhancing student engagement in the task.

SUMMARY

A performance task may be adjusted to make it more reflective of the school's curriculum, or more suitable to a group of students, or to reflect conditions in a particular setting.

ADJUSTING THE RUBRIC

If a task is adjusted to reflect a district's curriculum, to be more suitable to a group of students, or to be made more relevant, the rubric will probably also require adaptation. The extent to which such adaptation is needed will depend, of course, on the amount of adjustment done to the task itself.

ADAPTING THE CRITERIA

If the task is changed, the original criteria may no longer apply. The task may now encourage students to exhibit knowledge, skill, or understanding that were not part of the original task. If so, criteria related to these features should be added. Alternatively, elements of the original task may have been dropped; if so, the criteria corresponding to those elements should also be eliminated.

ADJUSTING THE PERFORMANCE DESCRIPTIONS

When a task is changed, particularly if the evaluation criteria are also changed, the performance descriptions may also require adjustment. Occasionally, the performance descriptions need adjustment even when no change was made in the task itself.

♦ If the level of difficulty of a task has been changed, either by altering the cognitive demands of the directions or by splitting it into several discrete tasks, the performance descriptions, even for the same criteria, may no longer be suitable. The descriptions may require revision to reflect the changed demands of the task.

♦ Even if the task has not been changed, but it is now being used with students who are more or less advanced than those for whom it was designed, the performance descriptions may need revision. Sometimes this can be accomplished by simply shifting the descriptions one place to the right or the left; that is, the description that was a 3 is now a 2, that which was a 4 is now the 3, and a new description is written for the 4.

♦ If the task has been revised to reflect a particular situation (for example, calculating wall area for paint instead of floor area for carpeting), the performance descriptions may need revision to reflect the changes. On the other hand, they may not need revision, depending on how they were written in the first place. Clearly, the more generic they are, the less revision they will need. But if the rubric has been written to be highly task-specific, substantial changes will be needed to reflect a different context.

SUMMARY

If a performance task is adjusted to make it more suitable for a group of students, its scoring rubric will almost certainly require a parallel change. Even if the task is not changed, educators may find that they want to adjust the rubric to better match the skills of their students or the criteria important to them.

PILOTING WITH STUDENTS

No adaptation of a performance task and its rubric is complete without trying it with students. Generally, all performance tasks (even those that are not adaptations of existing tasks) are revised somewhat after this pilot; certainly the scoring rubrics are revised in light of actual student work. The questions to be answered as a result of this pilot are summarized in the following material.

ENGAGEMENT

Are students engaged in the task? In the course of revision, did the task become irrelevant and boring to students? Does the task, if possible, reflect authentic applications of knowledge and skill?

ELICITING DESIRED KNOWLEDGE AND SKILL

Does the task, as revised, elicit the desired knowledge and skill from students? Occasionally, when tasks are revised, they lose their essential nature, so that students can complete the task without demonstrating the critical knowledge and skill in which their teachers are interested. This is most likely to happen if the student directions have been substantially revised.

CLARITY OF STUDENT DIRECTIONS

Are the directions to the students clear? In particular, if students' work will be evaluated according to specific criteria, have students been informed about those criteria in the directions themselves?

INDIVIDUAL ASSESSMENT

Does the task still permit the assessment of individual students? Or have the teachers, in the interests of making the task more relevant to a particular group of students or to a unique situation, also introduced group work that obscures the contribution of individuals?

TECHNICAL FEATURES OF THE RUBRIC

Does the scoring rubric, as revised, still meet all the technical requirements described in Chapter 6? Do the descriptions of levels of performance use vivid words, and avoid comparative language? Are the points on the scale approximately equidistant apart? Do the criteria reflect the most important aspects of performance?

Only an actual pilot of the revised task enables unambiguous answers to these questions. However, as educators and their students become more experienced in the use of performance tasks, this step may be combined with the first actual use of the task to evaluate student learning. That is, the task may be adapted as needed and used with students. Then, if it becomes apparent that the adaptation did not avoid the pitfalls described above, the actual scores awarded to students can be adjusted accordingly. For example, if student performance is poor, but it becomes clear that the principal reason for the poor performance relates to lack of clarity in the directions, then the teacher's evaluation of student mastery must reflect that difficulty.

SUMMARY

The final step in adapting an existing performance task and rubric is its actual pilot with students. Only then can educators be sure that it accomplishes their desired purposes.

8

PRIMARY SCHOOL MATHEMATICS PERFORMANCE TASKS

    This chapter has a collection of performance tasks and rubrics that are aligned with the mathematics standards, and that address all the important topics in primary school mathematics. They are arranged in alphabetical order (by title), with a table at the beginning of the chapter to assist you in locating tasks that you may want to use to assess specific skills and concepts. Some of the tasks include student work, which serves to illustrate the manner in which students interpret the directions given to them and to anchor the different points in the scoring rubrics.

    You may find that the tasks are useful as presented. Alternatively, you may find that they can serve your purposes better if you adapt them. One way of adapting tasks is to incorporate names of people and places familiar to students in your class. This practice is frequently amusing to students, and therefore engaging.

Task \ Standard	Number Operations Computation	Geometry & Measurement	Functions & Algebra
All in My Family	✓		
Amazing Equations	✓		✓
Book Order Shopping	✓		✓
Data Collecting	✓		
Detective Glyph	✓		
Everyday Math Journals	✓		
Extended Number Patterns	✓		
Fair Shares	✓		✓
Holiday Dinner	✓		✓
In Only a Minute	✓	✓	
Is It 15?	✓	✓	✓
Linear Patterns			
Losing Teeth	✓		✓
Measure Me	✓	✓	
Paper Quilts		✓	
Pizza Night	✓		✓
Probably Fair	✓		
The Same Size As Me	✓	✓	
Shapes in My World	✓	✓	✓
Story Problems	✓	✓	✓

Patterns & Relationships	Statistics Probability	Reasoning, Problem Solving	Mathematical Skills &Tools	Mathematics Communication
✓		✓		✓
✓		✓		✓
		✓	✓	✓
	✓	✓	✓	✓
		✓	✓	✓
✓		✓		✓
		✓		✓
		✓		✓
		✓		✓
		✓	✓	✓
		✓		✓
✓		✓		✓
	✓	✓		✓
		✓	✓	✓
		✓		✓
		✓		✓
	✓	✓	✓	✓
		✓	✓	✓
		✓	✓	✓
		✓		✓

In addition, tasks may be simplified or made more difficult by increasing or decreasing the amount of structure (or scaffolding) that students are provided. When you, the teacher, give guidance to students by outlining the steps needed in a solution, the resulting task is significantly easier (and less authentic). Similarly, when tasks are provided with considerable scaffolding, you can make them more complex by removing some or all of the scaffolding.

ALL IN MY FAMILY

MATHEMATICAL STANDARDS ASSESSED

- Number operations and concepts
- Patterns and relationships
- Problem solving and mathematical reasoning
- Mathematical communication

DIRECTIONS TO THE STUDENT

- Draw a picture of the people that live with you. How many people in your family? Include yourself _____
- How many eyes in your family? _____ How many fingers in your family? _____
- What else would you like to count? I counted
  _____
- What patterns did you notice?

Students are asked to illustrate their thinking, write an equation/number sentence and a few sentences to show and tell about their work.

MATHEMATICAL CONCEPTS

This task requires students to apply number counting patterns, by 2s, 5s, and 10s. Younger students may still need to use a one-to-one correspondence. Their illustrations give us insight to the process they have applied. Written equations and sentences support their thinking.

SOLUTION

Solutions vary according to the number of people in their family. Students are held accountable for an illustration, equation, and an idea of their own. Students may choose noses, toes, eyebrows, and so forth. More experienced students may notice patterns and relationships between hands and feet, ears and eyes, noses and mouths, and so forth.

SCORING GUIDE

	Level One	Level Two	Level Three	Level Four
Organization of Information	Random; doesn't represent the elements	Most of the elements are represented	All the elements of the problem are represented	Well-planned, attractive, representation of all the elements
Mathematical Accuracy	Major errors in computation and writing	Minor errors in computation or equation, no sentences	Correct illustration, equation and sentences	Challenging illustration, equation, and sentences
Explanation	Incomplete and invalid conclusions and communication	Communication reveals a partial understanding of number counting patterns and notation	Communication shows a basic understanding of number counting patterns and notation	Communication shows advanced application of number counting patterns and notation

LEVEL ONE

ALL IN MY FAMILY

Draw a picture of the people that live with you.

How many people in your family? __4__

How many eyes in your family? __8__

$6 + 1 = 7$

How many fingers in your family? __35__

What else would you like to count? I counted _____

_____

_____

This response represents four family members. It does not represent the number of eyes. The equation $6 + 1 = 7$ is not relevant. Only some of the fingers in the family were illustrated and counted. No additional idea was developed.

ALL IN MY FAMILY

Draw a picture of the people that live with you.

How many people in your family? _8_

How many eyes in your family? _16_

How many fingers in your family? _76_

What else would you like to count? I counted _threr are_
16 eyes in my family
ther are 8 Noses in my
family

$$16 + 8 = 23$$

This response represents eight family members, their eyes, and fingers. Minor errors are found in the computation of fingers and the equation 16 + 8 = 23. One-by-one counting of noses communicates a partial understanding of counting patterns.

LEVEL THREE

ALL IN MY FAMILY

Draw a picture of the people that live with you.

How many people in your family? 4 _____.

How many eyes in your family? 8 _____

How many fingers in your family? =40 _____

$1+1+1+1+1+1+1+1+1+1 =8$

$1+1+1+1+1+1+1+1+1 = 40$

What else would you like to count? I counted _____
I love my mom and Dad. _____

This response was difficult to evaluate. The work completed was accurate, but the student failed to answer the last question. The "I love my mom and dad" statement is typical of primary students who are so personally involved in their work, that they write comments that are not necessarily mathematical. During the oral presentation, the student was able to quickly self-correct, count the heads in the family, and report that there were four. The written equation demonstrates one-by-one counting.

LEVEL THREE

Draw a picture of the people that live with you.

How many people in your family? 6

How many eyes in your family? 12

How many fingers in your family? 60

30+30=60

What else would you like to count? I counted eye breal

becoes I chrid to have an eydea But
that was the oly one I can thee of.

2+2+2+2+2+2=12

This response is a solid three. The elements are represented; equations and sentences are accurate; and the presentation showed a basic understanding of counting patterns. (Jessica's fingers were not drawn but were counted.) The student writes, *"I counted eyebrows because I tried to have an idea but that was the only one I can think of."*

LEVEL FOUR

Draw a picture of the people that live with you.

How many people in your family? _5_

How many eyes in your family? _10_ .

$4 + 6 = 10$ $5 + 5 = 10$ $1+1+1+1+1+1+1+1+1+1 = 10$

How many fingers in your family? _50_

I cated my familys fingers.

$10 + 10 + 10 + 10 + 10 = 50$

What else would you like to count? I counted _How many fingers and how many eyes alltogather there are 60_

$50 + 10 = 60$

This response is well planned, detailed, and mathematically accurate. Notice the one-by-one counting and as well as the counting by 10s. The explanation revealed the student's understanding that counting by 1s would not be efficient with so many fingers; therefore, counting by 10s was applied.

AMAZING EQUATIONS

MATHEMATICAL STANDARDS ASSESSED

- ◆ Number operations and concepts
- ◆ Functions and algebra
- ◆ Patterns and relationships
- ◆ Problem solving and mathematical reasoning
- ◆ Mathematical Communications

DIRECTIONS TO THE STUDENTS

Choose a number between 8 and 20 (for first grade), 20 and 100 (for second grade), and 100 and 500 (for third grade). Record your number at the top of your paper.

Record at least 10 written equivalent equations for that number. You may draw pictures to illustrate your thinking. The equations can be written horizontally or vertically.

Share your equations with a partner.

MATHEMATICAL CONCEPTS

Teachers will want to model this activity for the whole group first. This task requires students to communicate their understanding of a numerical quantity and notation in written form. This activity can be used in math journals, from time to time, to show student progress through the school year.

SOLUTION

Solutions will vary. The quantity, quality, and accuracy of the equivalent equations will be evaluated. Require at least 10 equivalent equations for first grade, 15 for second grade, 20 for third grade. Encourage more capable students to work at a more challenging level with coins, clocks, and calculators. Students may use addition, subtraction, multiplication, division, or multistep problems.

SCORING GUIDE

	Level One	Level Two	Level Three	Level Four
Organization of Information	Random; difficult to follow	Format acceptable, most equations are easily read	Recorded required number of equations that can be easily read	Display includes vertical and horizontal equations and evidence of planning
Mathematical Accuracy	Does not apply numeric quantity, incomplete	Equations are mostly accurate and complete	Equations are accurate and complete	Accurate and complete; reflects varied approaches
Explanation	Unclear, shows little understanding of the concept	Minor errors in presentation; applied some numeric understanding	Clear explanation communicates numeric understanding	Well-presented; evidence of advanced mathematical reasoning

LEVEL THREE

$$27-1=26$$
$$28-2=26$$
$$25+1=26$$
$$26+0=26$$
$$1+55=26$$
$$27-1=26$$
$$33-6=26$$
$$6+20=26$$
$$20+6=26$$
$$19+7=26$$
$$7+19=26$$
$$0+10+6=26$$
$$9+9 5=26$$
$$5+5+5+5+6=26$$
$$6+6 8+6=26$$

$$0+26$$
$$17+8=26$$
$$1=26$$

Only a Level Three response is shown. This is a first grade
sample. The student generated many more examples than required. All but three are accurate. Notice the patterns in 6 + 20
= 26, 20 + 6 = 26. This student is applying the communicative
property of addition. The happy face before + 26 is really a
zero!

BOOK ORDER SHOPPING

MATHEMATICAL STANDARDS ASSESSED

- ◆ Number operations and concepts
- ◆ Functions and algebra
- ◆ Problem solving and mathematical reasoning
- ◆ Mathematical skills and tools
- ◆ Mathematical communication

DIRECTIONS TO THE STUDENT

Your aunt and uncle have just sent you a birthday card. They gave you a dollar for each year of your age. If you are six, they send you $6. If you are seven, they send you $7. If you are eight, they send you $8. If you are nine, they send you $9.

Your teacher has just given you a book order and you would like to buy some books. Look through the book order. Try to spend as much of the money you were given as you can. What can you buy? Remember that you can not spend more than the actual amount of money you received. What will you have left over?

You may use a calculator. Show your thinking.

MATHEMATICAL CONCEPTS

This task requires students to shop for a variety of books at different prices. They have a limited budget! Students may use calculators or computation skills. They are asked to show their work. Place value addition and subtraction skills, with or without regrouping, are being assessed. Older students may be given more money or asked to figure out several possible solutions to the problem.

SOLUTION

Solutions will vary according to the book order used and student choices. Credit is given to the combination of books that comes closest to the dollar amount without going over the limit. Students may need to be reminded not to exceed the limit. They must also report the remainder of money that wasn't spent.

AN ADDITIONAL BENEFIT!

Teachers are frequently bombarded with book orders from several different publishers. This is an activity that recycles the flyers!

SCORING GUIDE

	Level One	Level Two	Level Three	Level Four
Organization of Information	Random, no systematic approach	Hit and miss approach leads to some errors in record-keeping	Approach and work is mostly systematic	Well-planned, complete, and clearly displayed
Mathematical Accuracy	Major errors; large remainder; went over the limit or missing notation	Minor errors; <$1 remainder; missing notation	Computation and most of the notation is correct; <.75 remainder	Computation and all notation is correct; <.25 remainder
Explanation	Flaws indicate a lack of understanding of the concept	Work attempted leads to weak conclusions	Solution was reasonable and clearly communicated	Solution is well sequenced with options and a rationale

LEVEL ONE

clifford $1.95
The fat cat $1.95
The RugRats $ 195
A B Bag of tricks 1.95
Choose the bag of fun that's
right for your child 1 1.95

This response is simply a list of books that the student wanted. No attempt at computation was made. The student was given only $8.00 to spend.

LEVEL TWO

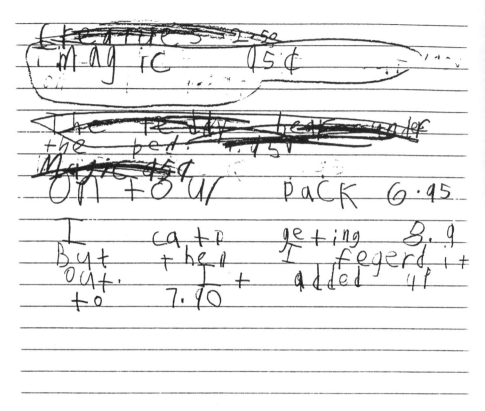

This response shows several attempts at spending $8.00. Finally, the student found something for $6.95 and added it on the calculator with $0.95. The student really struggled with the missing zero in the calculator display 8.9. Notation is missing. Solution was not clearly communicated

LEVEL THREE

McDuff comes Home 2.50
Kratts cretures wocky Animl
Facts 2.50
The Dumb Bunnies 2.50

2$+2$+2$ 5 1$+50¢ - 7$50¢

I spent 7$ ahd 5¢.
I irnde to uos a coklatr
I uost a coklatr
And my hed. I had 5o¢
left over.

This response is easy to follow. The student had $8 to spend. He found three books at $2.50 each. This student had not been taught a formal algorithm and so an inventive method was used. The student recorded the dollar sign after the dollar as we do for the cent sign.

Nyack College Library

LEVEL FOUR

The dumb Bunnies $2.50
Chameleons Are cool $2.50
Let,, my babies go $1.95
2+2+1+50+50+95 =6.95

I found three books two of
them costed 2.50 the other
one costed 1.95.
        I am 7 years old. I would hae
5¢ left over. I wish I was
8 years old so I could send more
money.

$2.50 +$1.95 +$2.50
(Chameleons   )
Are cool   )
Let, my   ↙)
Babies go   )
The Dumb   ↙ /
Bunnies
2+2+1+50+50+95=6.95

This response is complete and clearly displayed. This student
had $7 to spend. Computation and notation is correct, with a
remainder of five cents. Young children will frequently do
computation from left to right; hundreds, tens, and ones. This
child demonstrates his understanding of place value in his
equation notation. He wishes he were older so he'd have
more money to spend!

DATA COLLECTING

MATHEMATICAL STANDARDS ASSESSED

- ◆ Number operations and concepts
- ◆ Problem solving and mathematical reasoning
- ◆ Statistics and Probability
- ◆ Mathematical skills and tools
- ◆ Mathematical communication

DIRECTIONS TO THE STUDENTS

Today, each of us will have a chance to ask a question and collect data about something we're interested in learning about. We will graph our data using a bar graph and present our information in writing and orally to the class.

Choose a question you'd like to ask. Ask each person in our room. There are ___ students and ___ adults in our room today. (Record the total on the board.)

Decide how you will keep track of the answers. Would a yes/no list or a Venn Diagram help your organization?

Ask each person your question and keep track of the answers using your plan. Then create a bar graph showing your results. Remember to label your columns, rows, and to title your graph. When you have completed your graph, write two "I learned" statements about your data.

Oral Presentation: Tell us what your question was and how you collected the information. Show us your graph and tell us what you learned. Ask your classmates to share any questions or comments they may have.

MATHEMATICAL CONCEPTS

This task requires students to collect, graph, and communicate information through a graphic, written, and oral presentation. They must choose an appropriate question and an effective method for collecting their data. Directions could be read out loud and posted for students to review. The teacher can evaluate each child's work when the students are sharing it with their peers.

SOLUTION

Solutions will vary depending on the types of questions, the methods for collecting the data, and the writing ability of the individual students. This is an excellent task for comparing strategies and graphic organization. Students will amaze you with the many, varied questions they ask.

SCORING GUIDE

	Level One	Level Two	Level Three	Level Four
Organization of Information	Misrepresented or incomplete; random; inconsistent	Mostly complete data; approach is not concise	Complete data; workable approach	Complete data; highly efficient collection strategy
Bar Graph Display	Unlabeled, inaccurate and incomplete	Untitled, unlabeled, representation attempted in nonstandard format	Has 2 of 3 title, columns, and rows labeled correctly; accurate	Neat, accurate, labeled, evidence of planning
Written Statement	Unrelated, unclear	1 statement: shows some understanding of process	2 statements: analysis shows understanding of process	At least 2 statements, analysis extends beyond numeric observations
Oral Presentation	Shows little understanding of the process	Errors in sequence, incomplete thoughts	General overview of process is mostly complete and accurate	Sequences activity, shows mastery of research process

LEVEL ONE

What is your favorite ice-cream?

Chocolate									
Vanilla									
Bubble Gum									
Cookie Dough									
Rocky Road									

I learned that more kids like Vanilla.

This response shows a random collection of information. With some teacher intervention, the student was able to graph the information. However, there are 19 answers on the collection page, and 21 on the graph. There is no title, and columns are not numbered. The written statement is accurate but limited in mathematical communication.

LEVEL TWO

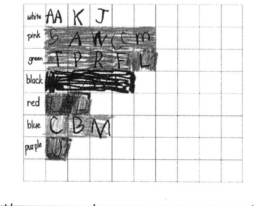

Hardly any body likes purple.

This student used the initials of the students she surveyed so that she could remember whom she had already polled. There is no systematic recording other than that the color matches the response. The graph is accurate, but missing a title and numbered columns. The written statement shows some understanding of the information collected.

LEVEL THREE

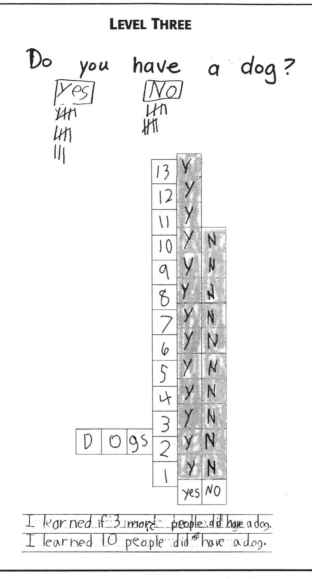

I learned if 3 more people did have a dog.
I learned 10 people did have a dog.

This response is a complete and organized collection of information. The bar graph is labeled with a title, columns and rows. The written statements reflect errors in thought that were clarified and self-corrected during the oral presentation. The student meant to say: "I learned that if three or more people did have a dog, *it would be tied*." Primary students don't always proof their written work. The oral explanations allow students a forum for editing their work.

LEVEL FOUR

have you had spider bites before?

yes
 卅卅Ⅰ

No
 卅卅ⅰ

11	🕷	✖		
10	🕷	✖	S	b
9	🕷	✖	p	i
8	🕷	✖	i	t
7	🕷	✖	d	c
6	🕷	✖	e	s
5	🕷	✖	r	
4	🕷	✖		
3	🕷	✖		
2	■	✖		
1	■	✖		
	yes	no		

I learned it was half and half
11 kids did not have a spider
bites and 11 kids did have
1 spider bites.

I learned there's a lot of
people that have spider
in their house because
there was a lot of peaple
that had spider bites.

This response is complete, accurate, and neat. The student made a pattern when she colored in the "no" responses and drew black spiders for the "yes" responses. The written statements demonstrate an understanding of fractions (*half and half*) and an analysis of where spiders come from *"in their house."*

DETECTIVE GLYPH

MATHEMATICAL STANDARDS ASSESSED

+ Number operations and concepts
+ Problem solving and mathematical reasoning
+ Mathematical skills and tools
+ Mathematical communication

DIRECTIONS TO THE STUDENT

In ancient times, stories were told with pictures. These pictures, sometimes found on cave walls, were called hieroglyphics. Together we're going to create a legend, using different attributes, that tells us something special about each of you. I will make a chart of the attributes we chose for us to follow when we create our art project. The project you will create is called a glyph.

When you have finished making your art project, write out three clues using the legend, to help your classmates figure out who you are.

MATHEMATICAL CONCEPTS

In this task, students are asked to represent, analyze, and interpret information from a legend or key. Although many ready-made idea books are available on the market, students may enjoy making up their own legends. Students will enjoy the challenge of being detectives, especially with a class across the hall. It will also discourage just remembering "who did what" during the activity.

This activity can also be used to sort, diagram, and graph group characteristics; for instance, boys who have brown eyes or girls who are seven.

SOLUTION

Solutions will vary according to the legend and seasonal thematic project you create with your students. Some attributes that can be included are: boy-girl, birthday, age, hobby, favorite food, favorite color, type of shoe, family members, ride-walk-bus to school, and eye color.

SCORING GUIDE

	Level One	Level Two	Level Three	Level Four
Construction of Glyph Model	Does not correspond to the legend	Mostly corresponds to the legend	Corresponds to the legend	Neat, creative, corresponds to the legend
Mathematical Accuracy	Inaccurate interpretation of the legend	Mostly correct interpretation of the legend	Accurate interpretation of legend data	Accurate interpretation leads to abstract conclusions
Written Response	Unclear, significant omissions	Shows an incomplete understanding of the process	Three complete and correct clues	Clues demonstrate a synthesis of all the information

On the next page is an example of a chart which lists the attributes of the glyphs. The attributes are selected by the students and the teacher together. Below the chart is an example of a student's drawing of a ladybird (or ladybug). The drawing indicates that the student does not like ladybirds (no circles at the end of the antennae); the student has never caught a ladybird (2 inch legs); and the student has been bitten by a bug (three dots).

Do you like ladybirds?

Yes \ /   No \ /

Have you ever caught a ladybird?

Yes *3" legs* No *2" legs*

Have you been bitten by a bug?

Yes *3 dots* No *2 dots*

Have you seen a _____ ladybird?

Red   Gray

Black   Yellow-green

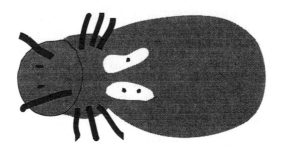

EVERYDAY MATH JOURNALS

MATHEMATICAL STANDARDS ASSESSED

- ◆ Number operations and concepts
- ◆ Problem solving and mathematical reasoning
- ◆ Patterns and relationships
- ◆ Mathematical communication

DIRECTIONS TO THE STUDENT

Keep a journal of five experiences outside of school that invited you to use mathematics. Date each entry. Tell what you were doing. Draw pictures, write an equation, and/or write a few sentences. What kind of mathematics did you do? Be ready to share with your classmates.

MATHEMATICAL CONCEPTS

This task requires students to justify, represent and discuss mathematical events in their daily life. From cooking to reading newspapers, we use numbers to count, measure, order, and so forth. Number sense develops through multiple experiences in our everyday life. To be motivated to learn more, students need to see the relationship and relevance of mathematics to *their* personal life. This task provides a rich opportunity for peer discussion.

Don't wait until the end of week to share! Have students share their work as they finish it so as to motivate other students to complete the assignment. Depending on what the students record, this task may also include geometry, measurement, patterns, and algebra.

SOLUTION

Solutions will vary. Each entry should have a date, the example of a mathematical task, and a connection to a mathematics strand.

SCORING GUIDE

	Level One	Level Two	Level Three	Level Four
Organization of Information	Random; incomplete	Acceptable format; mostly complete; <5 experiences	5 experiences that used math; dated; described	5 or more experiences; dated; described in detail; neat
Mathematical Accuracy	Misrepresented; incorrect	Minor flaws in the record-keeping	Accurately represented and supported by math concepts	Advanced math concepts applied and represented accurately
Explanation	Unclear; lacks relationship to mathematics	Some difficulty with interpretation; some events are recorded	Overview of task makes sense, clear understanding	Relates mathematical concepts and leads a rich discussion about experiences

EXTENDED NUMBER PATTERNS

MATHEMATICAL STANDARDS ASSESSED

- ◆ Number operations and concepts
- ◆ Patterns and relationships
- ◆ Problem solving and mathematical reasoning
- ◆ Mathematical communications

DIRECTIONS TO THE STUDENTS

Choose an inexpensive manipulative, such as a sticker, rubber stamp, pasta, or cereal. Notice something you would like to count by 2s, 5s, or 10s. Number your paper on the left side, from 1 to 6.

Arrange your objects on your paper from 1 to 6. Write a counting statement about what you notice. Write an equation that matches each of your statements.

(Older students can be asked to complete a 100 matrix and write the corresponding equations in addition or multiplication notation.)

MATHEMATICAL CONCEPTS

This task can apply to a wide range of student abilities. Younger students should have multiple whole-group experiences with real objects before they move to an abstract paper model. Whole-group practice will scaffold your students' ability to follow with independent work. This is a visual preparation for the multiplication model through repeated addition and patterning.

An oral presentation to the class or brief conference with a teacher allows the students to share their understandings.

SOLUTIONS

The students will need to complete the correct counting pattern for 2, 5, or 10. Children who are capable of more challenging work should be encouraged to work with other number patterns.

SCORING GUIDE

	Level One	Level Two	Level Three	Level Four
Organization of Information	Begins task without a plan; random visual display	Mostly complete information; acceptable format	Complete visual display numbered 1 to 6; statements and equations are accurate	Display is neat, complete, and well planned
Computational Accuracy	Major errors in computation; does not complete the process	Computation is mostly accurate; missing display or statements	Computation, statements, and equations are accurate	Advanced computation, statements, and equations are accurate
Oral Presentation or Conference	Unclear explanation; does not apply concept	Explanation shows an incomplete understanding of counting patterns	Mathematical terminology, visual model, and notation are clearly explained	Communicates clearly; applies information to share new insights on the project

LEVEL THREE

Star Extended Number Pattern

1 star has 5 points. 5+0=5

2 stars have 10 points. 5+5=10

3 stars have 15 points. 5+5+5=15

4 stars have 20 points. 5+5+5+5=20

5 stars have 25 points. 5+5+5+5+5 = 25

6 stars have 30 points. 5+5+5+5+5+5 =30

7 stars have 35 points. 5+5+5+5+5+5+5=35

8 stars have 40 points. 5+5+5+5+5+5+5+5=40

1	2	3	4	5	6	7	8	9	10
11	12	13	14	15	16	17	18	19	20
21	22	23	24	25	26	27	28	29	30
31	32	33	34	35	36	37	38	39	40
41	42	43	44	45	46	47	48	49	50
51	52	53	54	55	56	57	58	59	60
61	62	63	64	65	66	67	68	69	70
71	72	73	74	75	76	77	78	79	80
81	82	83	84	85	86	87	88	89	90
91	92	93	94	95	96	97	98	99	100

Only a three is shown. This response is an example of a three; a complete and accurate visual model of number counting patterns. Note the inclusion of the 100 matrix as additional support for the sentences and equations.

FAIR SHARES

MATHEMATICAL STANDARDS ASSESSED

- ◆ Number operations and concepts
- ◆ Problem solving and mathematical reasoning
- ◆ Functions and Algebra
- ◆ Mathematical communication

DIRECTIONS TO THE STUDENT

Your teacher has brought a bag of candy to share with the class. The students helped count the candy pieces. There are 106 pieces all together!

How many children are in your class? _____

How many pieces of candy will YOU get if everyone gets a fair share? _____

Show your thinking. Draw, write an equation, and write a few sentences that tell about your thinking.

MATHEMATICAL CONCEPTS

In this task, students are asked to identify the important elements of the problem and to illustrate their own model for division of a large quantity of candy. Primary students have not yet been introduced to formal algorithms for long division. Their strategies will reflect their number sense, procedural knowledge, and application of division with a likely remainder. This task can be easily modified for kindergarten students by reducing the number of pieces of candy in the bag.

SOLUTION

Solutions will vary depending on the class size. Some possible solutions are: 17 students—6 pieces with 4 left over; 18 students—5 pieces with 16 left over; 19 students—5 pieces with 11 left over; 20 students—5 pieces with 6 left over; 21 students—5 pieces with 1 left over; 22 students—4 pieces with 18 left over; 23 students—4 pieces with 14 left over; 24

students—4 pieces with 10 left over; 25 students—4 pieces with 6 left over.

Older students may enjoy the challenge of detecting the pattern in this activity.

SCORING GUIDE

	Level One	Level Two	Level Three	Level Four
Organization of Information	Random; disorganized; no representation of the problem	Graphic layout is difficult to follow; no visible solution	Graphic layout shows the solution to the problem	Evidence of planning; layout is a complete representation of the solution
Mathematical Accuracy	Major flaws in the equation and sentences	Minor errors in the equation and sentences	Equation and sentences are accurate	Equation and sentences demonstrate abstract thinking skills
Explanation	Minimal understanding of the division process required	Partial understanding leads to an incomplete conclusion	Demonstrates number sense and a possible solution to the problem	Presentation reflects a total rationale for the division process

LEVEL ONE

$10 + 10 + 10 = 30$

We would have 4 More left

Your teacher has brought a bag of candy to share with your class. The children have help count the candy pieces. There are 106 pieces all together!

How many children are in your class? ___22___

How many pieces of candy will you get if everyone gets a fair share? ___20___

Show your thinking.

This response is difficult to understand, random, and incomplete. The student began drawing 106 pieces of candy, tried numbering the pieces, and wrote an equation that is accurate but not relevant to the problem.

LEVEL TWO

FAIR SHARES

Your teacher has brought a bag of candy to share with your class. The children have help count the candy pieces. There are 106 pieces all together!

How many children are in your class? _____

How many pieces of candy will you get if everyone gets a fair share? _4_____

Show your thinking.

$5 +5 +5 +5 +5 +5 +5 +5 +5 +5 +5$
$+5 +5 +5 +5 +5 +5 +5 +5 +5 +5 +5$

This response has a drawing of 22 children and the pieces of candy that were passed out, one by one. The student didn't deal with the remainder and the equation on the back didn't match the solution.

LEVEL THREE

Your teacher has brought a bag of candy to share with your class. The children have help count the candy pieces. There are 106 pieces all together!

How many children are in your class? __22__

How many pieces of candy will you get if everyone gets a fair share? __5__

Show your thinking.

their is o lift

One of the people got 1 but he only Wont one.

This response shows the student's thinking, 22 student faces, and counting by 5s. When the student realized he would be over the amount, he solved the problem by giving the last child only 1. He further justified his answer by stating he only wanted one.

LEVEL THREE

Your teacher has brought a bag of candy to share with your class. The children have help count the candy pieces. There are 106 pieces all together!

How many children are in your class? __22__

How many pieces of candy will you get if everyone gets a fair share? __4__

Show your thinking.

I drew 22 X's.

I gave each X a piece, and another, and another 'till I was done. I had 17 left over.

This student drew 22 Xs to represent the children in the class. He gave each X a piece of candy, then another, and another until he was done. The equation doesn't equal 90 and the remainder is not 17. The student self-corrected during his explanation. Students will often need this presentation time to rethink their solutions and adjust their errors.

LEVEL FOUR

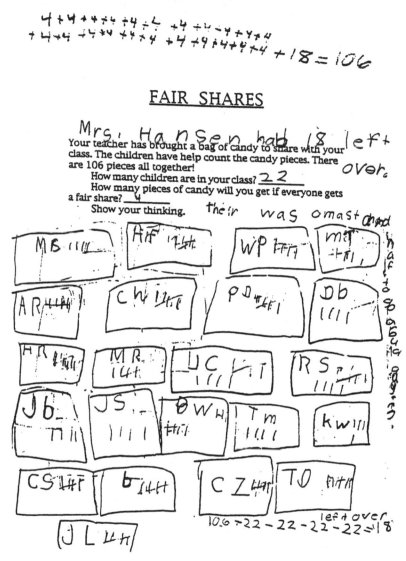

FAIR SHARES

Mrs. Hansen had 18 left over.

Your teacher has brought a bag of candy to share with your class. The children have help count the candy pieces. There are 106 pieces all together!

How many children are in your class? **22**

How many pieces of candy will you get if everyone gets a fair share? **4**

Show your thinking. their was omast enod

106 ÷ 22 − 22 − 22 − 22 − 22 = 18 left over

This response shows evidence of planning. The student used boxes, student initials, and tally marks. The equation at the top reflects addition and the one at the bottom reflects subtraction accurately. The student gave the teacher the large remainder, and also noticed, "There was almost enough to go around again."

HOLIDAY DINNER

MATHEMATICAL STANDARDS ASSESSED

- Number operations and concepts
- Functions and algebra
- Problem solving and mathematical reasoning
- Mathematical communication

DIRECTIONS TO THE STUDENT

Your extended family is coming to your house for the holidays. It's your job to set the table with a knife, fork, and spoon at each place setting. How many pieces of silverware will you need to set the table? Show and tell how you know.

I have _____ people coming to dinner.

I will need _____ pieces of silverware.

I know because _____.

MATHEMATICAL CONCEPTS

This task requires students to conclude how many people are in their extended family. They need to draw a model for an abstract concept (counting by three) without formal multiplication instruction. Some children will solve the problem with one-by-one counting; others may apply a counting pattern of three. Encourage young children to illustrate each member of their family and to use toothpicks or some other available manipulative to solve the task more concretely.

SOLUTION

Solutions will vary depending on the size of the extended family. Students enjoy doing this task around the seasonal holidays. Many of them actually have this chore in their home! They are amazed at how many pieces they have set. Credit is given for an illustration, an equation, and a sentence about their thinking.

SCORING GUIDE

	Level One	Level Two	Level Three	Level Four
Organization of Information	Random; major elements are not identified	Most of the major elements are identified	Reflects an appropriate strategy	Well-planned, highly efficient strategy
Mathematical Accuracy	Missing illustration, equation, and/or sentence	Mostly correct illustration, equation, and sentence	Correct illustration, equation, and sentence	Correct and completely clear illustration, equation, and sentences
Explanation	Minimal communication; conclusions are not valid	Attempt made; difficult to interpret work to final conclusion	Sequenced work leads to valid conclusions and understanding	Conclusion demonstrates application and synthesis of task

LEVEL ONE

Your extended family is coming to your
house for the holidays. It's your job to set
the table with a knife, fork and spoon at each
place setting. How many pieces of silverware
will you need to set the table? Show and tell
how you know.

I have __14__ people coming to dinner.

I will need __20__ pieces of silverware.

I know because I Counting bby 3th

$$3+3+3+3+3+k=14$$

This response exhibits minimal awareness of the major elements. Only three placemats are drawn. The answer, equation, and sentences are not valid.

LEVEL TWO

Your extended family is coming to your house for the holidays. It's your job to set the table with a knife, fork and spoon at each place setting. How many pieces of silverware will you need to set the table? Show and tell how you know.

I have __6__ people coming to dinner.

I will need __15__ pieces of silverware.

I know because

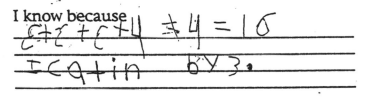

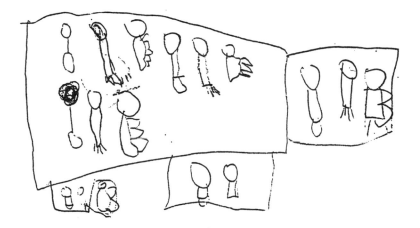

This response is mostly correct. The illustration supports the explanation but there's a piece missing on one of the place-mats, making the answer incorrect. The equation doesn't match the final conclusion.

LEVEL TWO

Your extended family is coming to your
house for the holidays. It's your job to set
the table with a knife, fork and spoon at each
place setting. How many pieces of silverware
will you need to set the table? Show and tell
how you know.

I have __12__ people coming to dinner.

I will need __33__ pieces of silverware.

I know because
Their weire 12 peOP l e.
ehey got a Kni f.fork and a
spoon.

3+3 +3+3=12

This response shows the major elements; people around a table and three tallies to represent the silverware. However,
one person did not get a set so the conclusion isn't accurate.
The equation is correct, but it doesn't match the problem.

LEVEL THREE

Your extended family is coming to your house for the holidays. It's your job to set the table with a knife, fork and spoon at each place setting. How many pieces of silverware will you need to set the table? Show and tell how you know.

I have __6__ people coming to dinner.

I will need __18__ pieces of silverware.

I know because
There are 6 people coming and
18 silverware altogether.
3+3+3+3+3+3=18

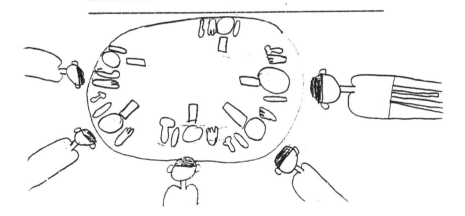

This response reflects an appropriate strategy with all the elements accurately represented. The equation and sentence leads to a valid conclusion and complete understanding.

LEVEL FOUR

Your extended family is coming to your
house for the holidays. It's your job to set
the table with a knife, fork and spoon at each
place setting. How many pieces of silverware
will you need to set the table? Show and tell
how you know.

I have __15__ people coming to dinner.

I will need __45__ pieces of silverware.

I know because

I conted by 3's.
And I conted the
Silverwer'

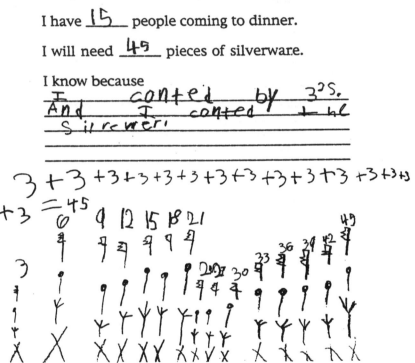

The student efficiently represented the 12 people with Xs and
then drew a fork, spoon, and knife above each X. He counted
by 3s and represented his strategy in an accurate equation
and sentence.

LEVEL FOUR

I have __18__ people coming to dinner.

I will need __54__ pieces of silverware.

I know because

_____ I counted by Threes
and I came up with 54.

I had alot of pepole in my
family to give Knife, fork,
and a Spoon?

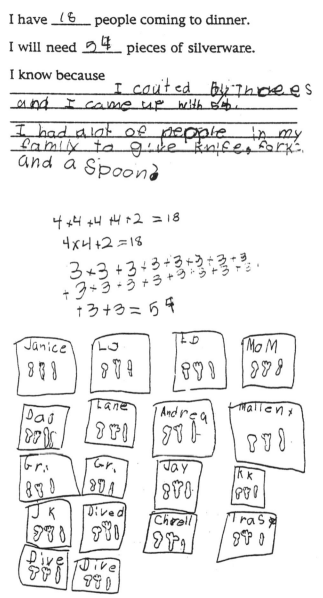

Detailed illustration shows evidence of planning and complete understanding of the problem. Equations include addition and multiplication. Excellent synthesis of the task.

IN ONLY A MINUTE

MATHEMATICAL STANDARDS ASSESSED

- Number operations and concepts
- Measurement
- Problem solving and mathematical reasoning
- Mathematical skills and tools
- Mathematical communication

DIRECTIONS TO THE STUDENTS

Using a stop watch, analog clock or sand timer, experience a minute (60 seconds).

Predict how many of these things you could do in only one minute:

I can tie my shoe.   Yes   No

I can say the ABCs.   Yes   No

I can build a tower of blocks.   Yes   No

I can clap my hands ____ times.

I can hop ____ times.

I can count to ____.

Think of four other things that you can do in just one minute. Have a partner verify your work. Record your work on your record sheet. All work should be neat and clearly labeled.

MATHEMATICAL CONCEPTS

This task requires students to estimate and predict a brief passage of time, personalize their own tasks, and justify their responses to a partner. Young children's reasoning is based on what they are seeing and experiencing—concrete, observable events. Qualitative time concepts are about sequencing events. Quantitative time is measured by clocks and calendars. Providing students with many opportunities to construct their own understanding about both of these abstract concepts is challenging.

SOLUTION

Solutions will vary according to the tasks chosen. Comparing results would allow for a rich discussion about each activity and about how speed and skill could be a variable in each child's results.

SCORING GUIDE

	Level One	Level Two	Level Three	Level Four
Organization of Information	Random; difficult to follow; incomplete	Mostly complete; acceptable format	10 statements completed; neat and labeled	Display is neat; complete and well-planned
Mathematical Accuracy	Answers are not validated by partner	Answers are mostly validated by partner	Answers are validated by partner	Validated; predictions and final outcomes show evidence of mastery
Explanation	Unclear; incomplete	Shows an incomplete understanding of time concepts	Communicates clearly; shows growth in understanding of time	Clear; concise; applies temporal understanding to presentation

Is it 15?

MATHEMATICAL STANDARDS ASSESSED

+ Number operations and concepts
+ Geometry and measurement
+ Functions and algebra
+ Problem solving and mathematical reasoning
+ Mathematical communication

DIRECTIONS TO THE STUDENT

Students will need to have had prior experiences with pattern blocks for this task.

> If the area of the green triangle is one, name the area of the other pattern blocks: the blue rhombus, the red trapezoid, and the yellow hexagon.

> Can you create two different designs with an area that equals exactly 15?

> How many pieces did you use on the first design? _____ The second? _____

> Do your designs have symmetry? _____

> What else did you notice? _____

> _____

> _____

Students are also asked to replicate their designs with colored paper shapes and to write an equation that illustrates their computation of an area of 15.

MATHEMATICAL CONCEPTS

This task asks students to determine the area of three pattern blocks based on a pre-determined standard unit. They need to apply that understanding to build two designs that have that exact area. Visual-spatial skills can also be assessed during the replication process. Rich discussions about symmetry and congruence take place during the sharing time.

Students also share their computation methods with one another.

SOLUTION

Solutions are varied and more creative than any adult could imagine! Students are held responsible for the questions on the worksheet, for two designs with a total area of 15, for a number sentence that explains their computation approach, and for the reconstruction of their design on paper. Younger children may struggle with the size of this task. It may be best to split it into several sessions.

SCORING GUIDE

	Level One	Level Two	Level Three	Level Four
Organization of Information	Random; no visible plan	Attempt at design, answers, and reproduction	Design, answers, and reproduction are complete	Neat, complete, and well-planned
Mathematical Accuracy	Major errors with area, design, and equation	Mostly accurate designs with an area close to 15; attempted equation	Correct application of area and equation	Application of area, design, and equation is clear and advanced
Explanation	Limited understanding of the concepts	Some parts of the process are represented	Demonstrates an understanding of the area concept	Synthesis of area task with rich mathematical language

LEVEL ONE

<u>IS IT 15?</u>
<u>Pattern Blocks Area</u>

If the area of the green triangle is one, name
the area of the other pattern blocks below.

_l_   2   3   6

Can you create two different designs with an
area that equals exactly 15?

How many pieces did you use on the first
design? _4_   The second? _3_

Do your designs have symmetry? _Yes_

What else did you notice? _21_ △
10   10   3 9

This response had major errors with area and symmetry. It
shows a limited understanding of the problem posed in this
task.

LEVEL TWO

IS IT 15?
Pattern Blocks Area

If the area of the green triangle is one, name
the area of the other pattern blocks below.

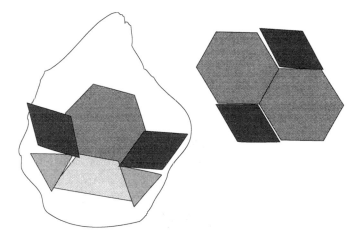

Can you create two different designs with an
area that equals exactly 15?

How many pieces did you use on the first
design? _6_ The second? _5_

Do your designs have symmetry? _Yes._

What else did you notice? _That it_
look like a robot with
no hido. It don't like
an eagle.

This response shows a partial understanding of area. The first
design has an area of 15, but the second has an area of 16. His
remarks about the first design read, *"That it looked like a robot
with no head,"* and the second design, *"It looked like an eagle."*

LEVEL THREE

IS IT 15?
Pattern Blocks Area

If the area of the green triangle is one, name
the area of the other pattern blocks below.

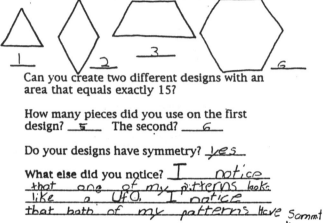

1   2   3   6

Can you create two different designs with an
area that equals exactly 15?

How many pieces did you use on the first
design? __5__ The second? __6__

Do your designs have symmetry? _yes_

What else did you notice? _I   notice_
that one of my patterns looks
like a U.F.O. I notice
that both of my patterns have Sammitry.

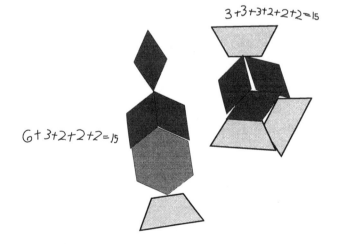

$$3+3+3+2+2+2=15$$

$$6+3+2+2+2=15$$

This response met the area requirements, demonstrated an
understanding of symmetry, and included correct equations.

LEVEL FOUR

IS IT 15?
Pattern Blocks Area

If the area of the green triangle is one, name the area of the other pattern blocks below.

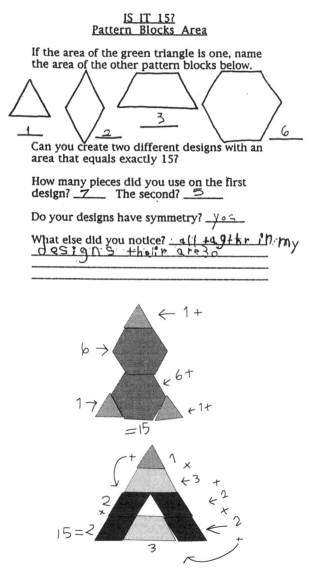

_1_ _2_ _3_ _6_

Can you create two different designs with an area that equals exactly 15?

How many pieces did you use on the first design? _7_ The second? _5_

Do your designs have symmetry? _Yes_

What else did you notice? _all together in my designs their are 30_

This response is clear, complete, and accurate. The explanation shows a synthesis of the task, an understanding of area and symmetry, and an interesting observation about the combined area of both designs.

LINEAR PATTERNS

MATHEMATICAL STANDARDS ASSESSED

- ◆ Patterns and relationships
- ◆ Problem solving and mathematical reasoning
- ◆ Mathematical communication

DIRECTIONS TO THE STUDENT

Using stickers, stamps, pasta, or cereal, create at least a 3-element pattern. Glue down your manipulative onto the strip of paper provided. Make your pattern repeat at least twice. Cover one of your pieces with a secret door.

When your pattern is finished, present it to the group. Read it aloud. Ask three of your peers to guess what they think is behind your secret door and why. Show your work. Name your pattern with letter names (ABC).

MATHEMATICAL CONCEPTS

This task requires students to organize a pattern, report their work, and facilitate a discussion with their peer group about alternative solutions and reasoning.

SOLUTIONS

Solutions will vary according to the developmental age of your students. Sequence or growth patterns could be a part of the more advanced students work. One-inch graph paper can also be used to show how patterns develop in a grid progression pattern.

SCORING GUIDE

	Level One	Level Two	Level Three	Level Four
Organization of Information	Random and incomplete	Linear organization is unclear	Repeated pattern two times in a linear format	Neatly done; evidence of planning and higher level reasoning
Mathematical Accuracy	Created design; no evidence of pattern	Minor flaw in representation; repeated once or only used 2 elements	Represented a 3-element pattern twice, accurately	Represented a 4–5-element pattern or growth pattern accurately
Oral Presentation	Unclear explanation; did not solicit peer responses	Explanation reveals only a partial understanding of the concepts	Reads pattern; asks peers appropriate questions and shares reasoning	Concise explanation; challenges peers and justifies reasoning

LOSING TEETH:
A STORY ABOUT AVERAGES

MATHEMATICAL STANDARDS ASSESSED

- ♦ Number operations and concepts
- ♦ Functions and algebra
- ♦ Statistics and probability
- ♦ Problem solving and mathematical reasoning
- ♦ Mathematical communication

DIRECTIONS TO THE STUDENTS

Ask at least four students in your class how many teeth they have lost. Record your loss, too. How many teeth is that all together? What is the average number of teeth lost for your group? How do you know? Explain your thinking. Compare your results to other groups in your class. What did you learn?

To complete this task you should:

- ♦ Determine a method to collect your information
- ♦ Represent the number of teeth lost by each member of your group with a white paper square
- ♦ Distribute the total number of teeth by the number of people in your group
- ♦ Conclude the average, or mean, number of teeth lost in your group

MATHEMATICAL CONCEPTS

This task requires students to design an inquiry with at least four other members of their class. Students then communicate what they understand about the mean or average. Students interpret their findings and compare them with other groups during the oral presentations. They are asked to make conclusions about the results of the task. Losing teeth makes a direct connection between living and learning for young children. One-centimeter or one-inch graph paper can be used as a manipulative to represent the number of teeth lost. Young children may need to physically divide whole numbers into fractions, others may deal with a remainder. Some students may want to draw a diagram.

SOLUTION

Solutions will vary depending on group size and the age of the students. Most samples will not have an even distribution of teeth, requiring students to demonstrate their understanding of fractional parts and/or remainders.

SCORING GUIDE

	Level One	Level Two	Level Three	Level Four
Organization of Information	Has difficulty choosing a strategy; random	Mostly complete and transferable data; <5 people	Visual model represents data collected; =5 people	Highly efficient strategy in data collection; >5 people
Mathematical Accuracy	Major errors in computation; reflects a limited mathematical understanding of averages	Reflects general understanding with minor errors; gaps in process	Correct calculations lead to reasonable conclusions about averages	Correct calculations lead to abstract conclusions about averages and group size
Explanation	No conclusions; unclear thought process	Incomplete understanding with weak conclusions	Accurate conclusions; demonstrates understanding of the process	Makes conclusions about the relationship of age, group size, and averages

LEVEL ONE

MY arch iS 14

This response is random, incomplete, and inaccurate. The student's conclusion: *"My answer is 14."*

LEVEL TWO

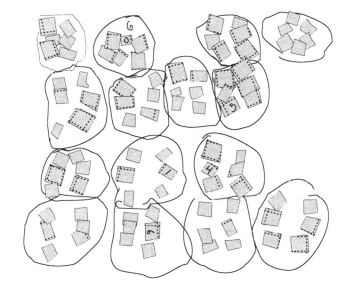

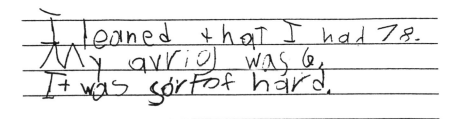

I leaned that I had 78.
My avriol was 6,
It was sorfof hard.

This student polled 15 people and concluded he had 78 teeth all together. He then averaged 90 teeth so he could put 6 in each group. There is no written equation or conclusion.

LEVEL THREE

21 teeth all together

I lrne that $8 + 8 + 4 + 1 = 21$

their Were 5 ekwo grops and 1 teeth loft ovr.

MY AYERAGE iS
for

This response is a sample of five people. The data collection strategy is visually clear and the concluding statements are accurate. One child lost 5 teeth, one lost 4, two children lost 2 teeth, and one child lost 8. *"I learned that 8 +8 + 4 +1 = 21. There were five equal groups and one teeth left over."*

LEVEL FOUR

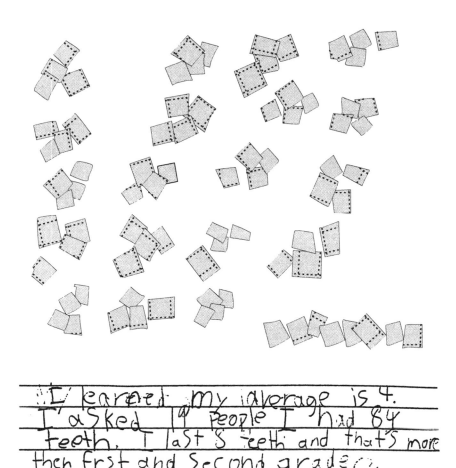

I learned my average is 4.
I asked 19 people I had 84
teeth. I last 5 teeth and that's more
then frst and second graders.

This visual model represents 19 students, with 4 teeth in each group, and a remainder of 8. The correct calculations lead to accurate conclusions about the process of averaging. The student also made an observation about the relationship of student grade levels.

MEASURE ME

MATHEMATICAL STANDARDS ASSESSED

- ◆ Number operations and concepts
- ◆ Geometry and measurement
- ◆ Problem solving and mathematical reasoning
- ◆ Mathematical skills and tools
- ◆ Mathematical communication

DIRECTIONS TO THE STUDENT

Have a friend trace your body on a large piece of paper. You can be a friend and trace their body, too! How many ways can we measure you? Choose a linear measurement unit and predict and measure at least five lengths. Record your guess and final check. Have your partner check your work.

MATHEMATICAL CONCEPTS

This task requires students to apply skills in measurement and calculation to a practical situation. The students need to measure, to a reasonable degree of accuracy, at least five linear dimensions and record their results. Provide optional standard and nonstandard units for measurement such as unifix cubes, tiles, toothpicks, learning links, rulers, tape measures, and yardsticks.

Young children are most comfortable with linear dimension. Depending on your district curriculum goals and your student's prior experiences, tasks that deal with weight, temperature, and volume could be useful for assessment purposes.

SOLUTION

Solutions will vary depending on the size and age of your group of students. The steps in the process should be modeled frequently. Experiences with multiple measurement instruments are critical for a child's understanding.

SCORING GUIDE

	Level One	Level Two	Level Three	Level Four
Approach	Disorganized; unfinished	Attempted display of self; record-keeping is hard to follow	Adequate display; record-keeping is easy to follow	Shows advanced planning; neat, well-represented record-keeping
Mathematical Accuracy	Major errors in estimation and in actual measurement skills	Minor errors in estimation and actual measurement skills	Estimation and actual measurement are close; tools and skills used correctly	Accurate predictions and demonstration of skills with a variety of tools
Explanation	Incomplete application of the linear measurement concept	Mostly complete understanding of the concept and the necessary steps	Clear understanding and application of linear measurement units	Creative; clear understanding of the variety of measurement tools available

PAPER QUILTS

MATHEMATICAL STANDARDS ASSESSED

- ♦ Geometry and measurement
- ♦ Problem solving and mathematical reasoning
- ♦ Mathematical communication

DIRECTIONS TO THE STUDENT

Decide which two colors of construction paper squares you will use to represent the two fields of color on the star quilt pattern. Glue the pieces onto the paper pattern provided, according to your key. You will want to cut your square pieces into triangles so that they will fit your quilt block pattern. Cut out the finished quilt square.

Answer these questions:

- ♦ How many triangles of color #1 did you use? ___
- ♦ How many triangles of color #2 did you use? ___
- ♦ How many triangles of both colors did you use all together? ___
- ♦ What is the square area of this quilt block? ___
- ♦ What is the perimeter of this quilt block? ___
- ♦ What else did you notice? Can you think of three other things?

MATHEMATICAL CONCEPTS

This task requires students to apply a key to a quilt design. Patterning, geometry, symmetry, area, and perimeter are also applied mathematical skills.

SOLUTIONS

There are two possible solutions to this activity if you only use two colors. Students may notice patterns, diagonal, vertical, and horizontal lines, angles, and so forth. Multiple opportunities exist with more than two color combinations and more complex quilt designs. This activity lends itself to sorting the completed quilt blocks, to building a class quilt with all the individual pieces, and to a lesson on area, perimeter, and factoring with older students.

SCORING GUIDE

	Level One	Level Two	Level Three	Level Four
Organization of Information	Application does not correspond to the key	Application is acceptable; difficulty with layout	Application corresponds with the color key	Corresponds to the color key; neat, fine-motor skills
Mathematical Accuracy	Incorrect answers to questions; visual model is confusing	Mostly correct answers to questions, visual model has minor errors	Correct answers to questions; visual model is accurate	Correct answers, accurate model, and attempt at factors, area, and perimeter
Application	No statements made that reflect observation of the quilt block	Less than 3 statements that correctly reflect observations of the quilt block	3 statements that correctly reflect observations of the quilt block	3 or more statements that show application of mathematical vocabulary

PIZZA NIGHT

MATHEMATICAL STANDARDS ASSESSED

- ♦ Number operations and concepts
- ♦ Functions and algebra
- ♦ Problem solving and mathematical reasoning
- ♦ Mathematical communication

DIRECTIONS TO THE STUDENT

You and your family have ordered one extra-large pizza for supper. The pizza is cut into 18 slices. How many slices will you get if everyone gets the same amount? Show and tell your work.

There are _____ members in my family.

I will get _____ slices of pizza.

MATHEMATICAL CONCEPTS

In this task, students are asked to illustrate their thinking and to write an equation and a few sentences about how they thought about the problem. Students can organize the information in a graphic format and demonstrate what they know about dividing up equal shares and fractions. Young students may need additional manipulative support and may prefer to be interviewed in lieu of the written assignment.

SOLUTION

Solutions will vary depending on the number of family members: 2 members will share 9 pieces each, 3 members will share 6 pieces, 4 members will share 4½ pieces, 5 members will share 3⅗ pieces, 6 members will share 3 pieces, 7 members will share 2⁴⁄₇ pieces, and 8 members will share 2¼ pieces. Students may want to justify giving the adults more, a real life adaptation, rather than work with the abstract fractions.

SCORING GUIDE

	Level One	Level Two	Level Three	Level Four
Organization of Information	Random; visual display is difficult to follow	Mostly complete; some elements are unclear	Visual display reflects the problem	All the elements of the problem are clearly identified
Mathematical Accuracy	Omission and serious errors led to invalid results	Minor flaws in graphic or equation may have led to error	Applications of the mathematical concepts are correct	Applications of the concepts, notation, and conclusions are advanced
Explanation	Serious gaps in understanding; inaccurate conclusion	Incomplete understanding of the application of division	Communicates an understanding of an appropriate division strategy	Uses mathematical vocabulary and applies the division concept

LEVEL ONE

You and your family have ordered one extra-large pizza for supper. The pizza is cut into 18 pieces. How many pieces will you get if everyone gets the same amount? Show and tell your work.

There are __4__ members in my family.

I will get __5⅓__ pieces of pizza.

MY F⅓ G 4 PIZ² · I like a loooo pizza.

8 + 5⅓ = 60

This response is random and difficult to follow. The statements and equations do not match the conclusion to this problem.

LEVEL TWO

You and your family have ordered one extra-large pizza for supper. The pizza is cut into 18 pieces. How many pieces will you get if everyone gets the same amount? Show and tell your work.

There are __4__ members in my family.

I will get __4__ pieces of pizza.

I had 4 in a hafa So did mY famaY.

$4 + 4 = 4$ $1 + 1 + 1 + 1 + 1$ $= 1$

This response shows the pizza, the four members of the family, and the beginnings of understanding division. "I had 4 in a hafa so did my famay." However, the equation doesn't match the illustration or explanation.

LEVEL TWO

You and your family have ordered one extra-large pizza for supper. The pizza is cut into 18 pieces. How many pieces will you get if everyone gets the same amount? Show and tell your work.

There are __6__ members in my family.

I will get __2__ pieces of pizza.

6 lift ovr and my family

I corid by 2s

This response is an example of a minor flaw that leads to an inaccurate conclusion. The student did not follow through with the remaining pieces. There is a clear graphic display, the sentence supports the conclusion, and there is evidence of counting by 2s. So close!

LEVEL THREE

You and your family have ordered one extra-large pizza for
supper. The pizza is cut into 18 pieces. How many pieces will
you get if everyone gets the same amount? Show and tell
your work.

There are __4__ members in my family.

I will get __4__ pieces of pizza.

I would get 4 becuse 4+4+5x'5=
18 I conted by 4's. be 6 but it
I thoght it would be 6 but it
is 18
roobii's over there

I desited the kids sheed get 4
a the adolts sheed ged 5,

This response displays all the elements of the problem. The
conclusion, *"I decided the kids should get 4 and the adults should
get 5"* is a real-life explanation for the remainder.

LEVEL FOUR

You and your family have ordered one extra-large pizza for supper. The pizza is cut into 18 pieces. How many pieces will you get if everyone gets the same amount? Show and tell your work.

There are __4__ members in my family.
I will get __4 1/2__ pieces of pizza.

Mom

Dad

~~H~~ane

me

no more ↓

4 x 4 + 2 / 1 = 4 1/2

I had to cot the two pesie in hafe of one. we got Four pesis and a hafe

---

This response clearly demonstrates the student's understanding of division and fractions. The student writes, "*I had to cut the two pieces in half, so we got four pieces and a half of one.*"

LEVEL FOUR

You and your family have ordered one extra-large pizza for supper. The pizza is cut into 18 pieces. How many pieces will you get if everyone gets the same amount? Show and tell your work.

There are __6__ members in my family.

I will get __3__ pieces of pizza.

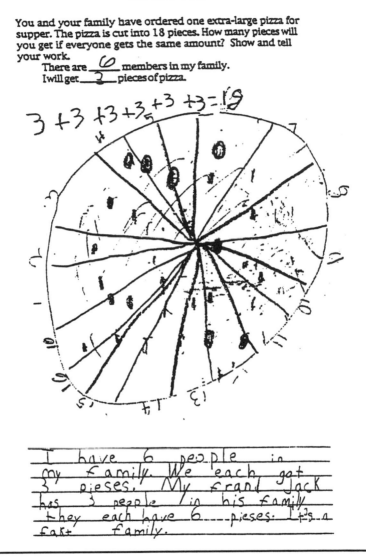

$$3 + 3 + 3 + 3 + 3 + 3 = 18$$

I have 6 people in my family. We each got 3 pieses. My Grand Jack has 3 people in his family they each have 6 pieses. It's a fact family.

This response identifies all the elements of the problem. The student asked us to disregard the original numbers outside the pizza. This student was working next to another student who had three people in his family. As the two were thinking out loud and counting, he noticed the relationship between the two answers (3×6, 6×3). *"It's a fact family"* was his explanation for the communicative property of multiplication.

PROBABLY FAIR

MATHEMATICAL STANDARDS ASSESSED

- ♦ Number operations and concepts
- ♦ Statistics and probability
- ♦ Problem solving and mathematical reasoning
- ♦ Mathematical communication

DIRECTIONS TO THE STUDENT

When you play a game with a spinner, you usually have an equal or fair chance of winning. Design a spinner for you and your partner that would probably be fair for both of you. Spin it 10 times and record your results.

Design a second spinner that would give you an advantage to win. Spin it 10 times and record your results.

Compare your results from both experiments. What did you learn?

MATHEMATICAL CONCEPTS

Primary students believe that their world should be fair. Multiple game experiences with spinners and dice allow them to construct their own understanding of probability and draw conclusions about luck and chance.

Students working in pairs can validate each other's predictions and verify accurate recordkeeping.

You can use index paper or card stock for the spinner face, paper clips and brads for the spinner components.

For additional practice, have students pair up with other partners and record the data. How did the results compare to the first experiment?

SOLUTION

Solutions will vary slightly on the fair spinners. A class graph of the pair results would provide a rich discussion about probability.

The unfair spinner solutions will vary greatly to the delight of the winners. Group results can also be posted. Student comments may be recorded and labeled along side the spinners and graph displays.

SCORING GUIDE

	Level One	Level Two	Level Three	Level Four
Organization of Information	Incomplete; difficult to follow	Mostly a complete attempt at a design and data	Complete design and data collection	Evidence of planning; neat; complete design and data
Mathematical Accuracy	Major errors and omissions	Minor errors lead to flaws in outcomes	Transfer of information is believable	Challenging problem is posed and executed
Explanation	Unclear; little application of the probability	Shows some application of probability	Communicates an understanding of probability	Application and synthesis of probability and statistics

THE SAME SIZE AS ME

MATHEMATICAL STANDARDS ASSESSED

- Number operations and concepts
- Measurement
- Problem solving and mathematical reasoning
- Mathematical skills and tools
- Mathematical communication

DIRECTIONS TO THE STUDENT

Use cotton string to measure the circumference (that is, the distance around) your head. Measure right across your ears and forehead. Have a friend check your work. Record your results. Compare your measurement with your partner's. Whose circumference is longer? Are they the same? Record your results.

Find someone else in the room who measures the same as you. Record your results.

Look around the classroom. Use your string. Can you find five people or things that measure the same as you? Record your results.

MATHEMATICAL CONCEPTS

This task requires students to use tools to measure their head circumference and to help a partner measure his or hers. Students also compare their results to other students, their classroom environment, and their own body. Estimation and recordkeeping are also being assessed.

Metric and U.S. Customary units can be used for practice with standard units of measurements. Cotton string or cord is best to avoid "stretching" in materials like yarn.

SOLUTION

Solutions will vary depending on the size and age of your class. The vocabulary and process should be modeled frequently with thematic applications to pumpkins, snowmen, animals, globes, gym balls, and so forth.

SCORING GUIDE

	Level One	Level Two	Level Three	Level Four
Organization of Information	Incomplete; difficult to follow	Mostly complete with some systematic attempt	Complete data with systematic approach	Evidence of planning; clear, concise, and varied data
Mathematical Accuracy	Measurements are not valid	Measurements are + or - 2 inches or centimeters	Measurements are valid, + or - ½ inch or centimeter	Measurements are valid and challenging
Explanation	Unclear; little application of the measurement process	Shows some application of measurement skills	Complete understanding of the skills and tools necessary to measure	Application and synthesis of measurement and use of circumference

SHAPES IN MY WORLD

MATHEMATICAL STANDARDS ASSESSED

- ◆ Patterns and relationships
- ◆ Geometry
- ◆ Problem solving and mathematical reasoning
- ◆ Mathematical communication

DIRECTIONS TO THE STUDENT

Identify the shapes you'll be looking for:

Kindergarten: Circle, square, rectangle, triangle
First Grade: Oval, trapezoid, diamond, rhombus
Second Grade: cone, sphere, cylinder, cube, and
prism

Can you find at least three examples of each of those shapes in your classroom (home or outdoor area)?

Record your ideas in pictures and/or writing. Share with your friends.

MATHEMATICAL CONCEPTS

This task encourages students to look in their real world environments in school, at home, and outdoors, for common two- and three-dimensional shapes. This task can be modified for each grade level depending on the curriculum objectives. Check your district requirements.

Young children may feel more comfortable drawing pictures of the objects and labeling them. A ball may be represented as "BL." A round circle placed by the letters may help you read the work and stimulate the child's memory about the shape. The pictures provide support for their writing and presentation.

Patterns and relationships in nature can provide a rich setting for this task. This task can be repeated several different times during the year to show student growth and progress.

SOLUTION

Solutions will vary depending on the required shapes and the environment. Students will identify, categorize, and describe common geometric figures and draw conclusions about the relationship of shapes in their world.

SCORING GUIDE

	Level One	Level Two	Level Three	Level Four
Organization of Information	Record-keeping is random	Incomplete record-keeping	Complete record-keeping	Evidence of systematic record-keeping
Mathematical Accuracy	Pictures and writing do not support ideas	Minor errors in pictures and writing; <3 examples	3 examples clearly represented	>3 examples; varied application
Presentation	Explanation is unclear	Mostly clear thoughts about shapes in the world	Complete understanding of names and shapes in the world	Advanced application and vocabulary about shapes

STORY PROBLEMS

MATHEMATICAL STANDARDS ASSESSED

- ◆ Number operations and concepts
- ◆ Functions and Algebra
- ◆ Problem solving and mathematical reasoning
- ◆ Mathematical communication

DIRECTIONS TO THE STUDENT

Today, each of us will create a story problem. You will use the storyboards and counters provided to make your story.

Your story must match your storyboard picture. Think of a mathematical question you could ask about your picture.

Write an equation/number sentence that reflects your math question. Include the answer.

Be ready to present your story problem to the class.

MATHEMATICAL CONCEPTS

The children will need time to explore with the materials they will be using. Allow students time to share their own initial stories orally with a partner. Teachers can model sample story problems for practice. Students will solve them on their own storyboard while the teacher repeats the problem. The children will share their solutions with each other. After this introductory lesson, children will be ready to create their own storyboards. Students can write their own stories or dictate them to an adult.

When the students share their stories with the class, other students will want to solve the posed problem using manipulatives, pictures, numbers, or words. Many approaches are valued. Teachers can evaluate the project at the time of student oral presentation.

SOLUTIONS

Answers will vary according to the story problems the students pose. Teachers should pose more challenging missing addend or subtrahend, comparing, multiplication, and division problems, so that the students can authentically demonstrate their understanding of mathematics through creative, inventive, problem-solving solutions.

Teachers can introduce one given number for a whole group lesson and challenge students to come up with a representation of that quantity in addition or subtraction stories. This story-telling lesson allows students to see the relationship between addition and subtraction operations ($7 + 1 = 8$ and $8 - 1 = 7$). Encourage students to represent subtraction in other than removal methods, as in missing addend and comparing models.

Student stories might reflect the number quantity and operation in the grade-level instruction goals. For example:

Kindergarten students may be working on number sense from 1 to 5

First graders may be working on addition and subtraction facts to 10

Second graders may be working on addition and subtraction facts to 20

Third graders may be working on multiplication of one-digit numerals

SCORING GUIDE

	Level One	Level Two	Level Three	Level Four
Organization of Information	Picture or story is unfinished	Story doesn't match picture	Story matches picture	Story matches picture; evidence of planning
Posing a Question	Does not ask a question; may make a statement	Incompatible question; doesn't match picture or have mathematical language	Poses a simple computation question: How many all together? How many are left?	Poses a higher level question: fewer than; greater than; multiple steps
Written Equation	No equation	Incorrect equation or answer	Correct number sentence notation and answer	Challenging equation is written using age appropriate notation
Oral Presentation	Reveals no observable sequence	Errors in sequence; omits information; has an incorrect number sentence or answer	Correctly sequenced; number sentence and answer are correct	Correct work; communicates in complete thoughts with mathematical vocabulary

LEVEL TWO

It was snowing and there were
10 snowmen and 6 more went sliding
and 4 mittens stad home with the
other 10 how mene stad home?

This response doesn't match the picture or have a completed equation or an answer.

LEVEL THREE

Once upon a time there were s.three
snowmen sleding and there were four
mittens on the line drying and santa man
was flying in his sledd. How many
snowmen all together 3+3=? [6]

This response has a story that matches the picture, a math question, equation and correct answer with notation. One of the snowmen is "Santaman." The student also included unnecessary information in the story problem.

LEVEL FOUR

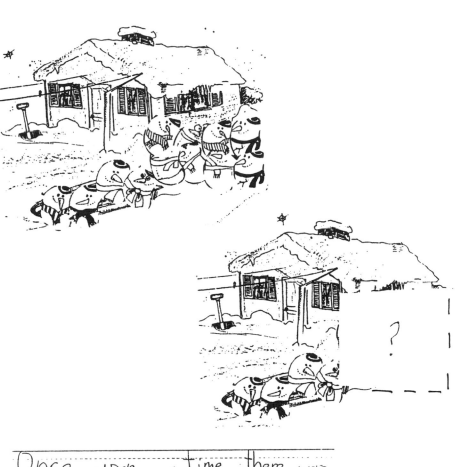

Once upon a Time there were
12. 4 snow men went sleding at
Lions park. The rest stayed home
and drank hot choklit. How
many drank hot choklit? 12-4=8

This response shows evidence of planning. The student poses
a missing addend question using a secret door. It has a correct
sentence and answer.

APPENDIX

STUDENT HAND-OUTS

Please feel free to photocopy the material in this
Appendix and distribute it to your students.

ALL IN MY FAMILY

Name: _____

Directions:

Draw a picture of the people that live with you.

How many people in your family? Include yourself. _____

How many eyes in your family? _____

How many fingers in your family? _____

What else would you like to count? I counted
_____
_____
_____
_____

What patterns did you notice?

AMAZING EQUATIONS

Name: _____

Directions:

Choose a number between _____ and _____.

Record your number_____.

Record at least 10 written equivalent equations for that number. You may draw pictures to illustrate your thinking. The equations can be written horizontally or vertically.

Share your equations with a partner.

BOOK ORDER SHOPPING

Name: _____

Directions:

Your aunt and uncle have just sent you a birthday card. They gave you a dollar for each year of your age. If you are six, they send you $6. If you are seven, they send you $7. If you are eight, they send you $8. If you are nine, they send you $9.

Your teacher has just given you a book order and you would like to buy some books. Look through the book order. Try to spend as much of the money you were given as you can. What can you buy? Remember that you can not spend more than the actual amount of money you received. What will you have left over?

You may use a calculator. Show your thinking.

DATA COLLECTING

Name: _____

Directions:

Today, each of us will have a chance to ask a question and collect data about something we're interested in learning about. We will graph our data using a bar graph and present our information in writing and orally to the class.

Choose a question you'd like to ask. Ask each person in our room. There are _____ students and _____ adults in our room today. The total is _____.

Decide how you will keep track of the answers. Would a yes/no list or a Venn Diagram help your organization?

Ask each person your question and keep track of the answers using your plan. Then create a bar graph showing your results. Remember to label your columns, rows, and to title your graph. When you have completed your graph, write two "I learned" statements about your data.

Oral Presentation: Tell us what your question was and how you collected the information. Show us your graph and tell us what you learned. Ask your classmates to share any questions or comments they may have.

DETECTIVE GLYPH

Name: _____

Directions:

In ancient times, stories were told with pictures. These pictures, sometimes found on cave walls, were called hieroglyphics. Together we're going to create a legend, using different attributes, that tells us something special about each of you. I will make a chart of the attributes we chose for us to follow when we create our art project. The project you will create is called a glyph.

When you have finished making your art project, write out three clues using the legend, to help your classmates figure out who you are.

EVERYDAY MATH JOURNALS

Name: _____

Directions:

Keep a journal of five experiences outside of school that invited you to use mathematics. Date each entry. Tell what you were doing. Draw pictures, write an equation, and/or write a few sentences. What kind of mathematics did you do? Be ready to share with your classmates.

EXTENDED NUMBER PATTERNS

Name: _____

Directions:

Choose a manipulative such as a sticker, rubber stamp, pasta, or cereal. Notice something you would like to count by 2s, 5s, or 10s. Number your paper on the left side, from 1 to 6.

Arrange your objects on your paper from 1 to 6. Write a counting statement about what you notice. Write an equation that matches each of your statements.

FAIR SHARES

Name: _____

Directions:

Your teacher has brought a bag of candy to share with the class. The students helped count the candy pieces. There are 106 pieces all together!

How many children are in your class? _____

How many pieces of candy will YOU get if everyone gets a fair share? _____

Show your thinking. Draw, write an equation, and write a few sentences that tell about your thinking.

HOLIDAY DINNER

Name: _____

Directions:

Your extended family is coming to your house for the holidays. It's your job to set the table with a knife, fork, and spoon at each place setting. How many pieces of silverware will you need to set the table? Show and tell how you know.

I have _____ people coming to dinner.

I will need _____ pieces of silverware.

I know because:

IN ONLY A MINUTE

Name: _____

Directions:

Using a stop watch, analog clock or sand timer, experience a minute (60 seconds).

Predict how many of these things you could do in only one minute:

I can tie my shoe.   Yes   No

I can say the ABCs.   Yes   No

I can build a tower of blocks.   Yes   No

I can clap my hands _____ times.

I can hop _____ times.

I can count to _____.

Think of four other things that you can do in just one minute. Have a partner verify your work. Record your work on record sheet. All work should be neat and clearly labeled.

Is it 15?

Name: _____

Directions:

> If the area of the green triangle is one, name the area of the other pattern blocks below.

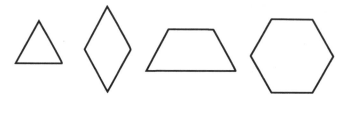

_____   _____   _____   _____

> Can you create two different designs with an area that equals exactly 15?
>
> How many pieces did you use on the first design? _____ The second? _____
>
> Do your designs have symmetry? _____
>
> What else did you notice?

LINEAR PATTERNS

Name: _____

Directions:

Using stickers, stamps, pasta, or cereal, create at least a 3-element pattern. Glue down your manipulative onto the strip of paper provided. Make your pattern repeat at least twice. Cover one of your pieces with a secret door.

When your pattern is finished, present it to the group. Read it aloud. Ask three of your peers to guess what they think is behind your secret door and why. Show your work. Name your pattern with letter names (ABC).

LOSING TEETH:
A STORY ABOUT AVERAGES

Name: _____

Directions:

Ask at least four students in your class how many teeth they have lost. Record your loss, too. How many teeth is that all together? What is the average number of teeth lost for your group? How do you know? Explain your thinking. Compare your results to other groups in your class. What did you learn?

To complete this task you should:

- Determine a method to collect your information
- Represent the number of teeth lost by each member of your group with a white paper square
- Distribute the total number of teeth by the number of people in your group
- Conclude the average, or mean, number of teeth lost in your group

MEASURE ME

Name: _____

Directions:

Have a friend trace your body on a large piece of paper. You can be a friend and trace their body, too! How many ways can we measure you? Choose a linear measurement unit and predict and measure at least five lengths. Record your guess and final check. Have your partner check your work.

PAPER QUILTS

Name: _____

Directions:

We will each construct a star quilt pattern for a class quilt project. Decide which two colors of construction paper squares you will use to represent the two fields of color. Glue the pieces onto the paper pattern provided, according to your key. You will want to cut your square pieces into triangles so that they will fit your quilt block pattern. Cut out the finished quilt square.

Answer these questions:

- How many triangles of color #1 did you use? ___
- How many triangles of color #2 did you use? ___
- How many triangles of both colors did you use all together? ___
- What is the square area of this quilt block? ___
- What is the perimeter of this quilt block? ___

What else did you notice? Can you think of three other things?

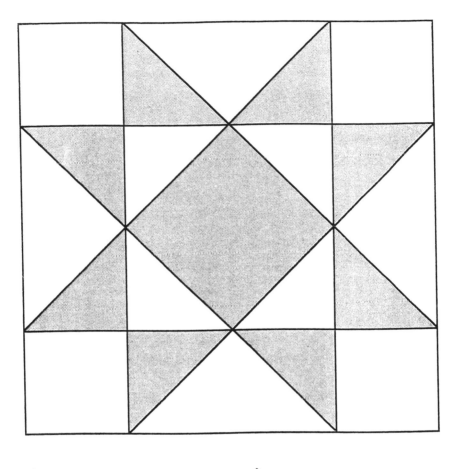

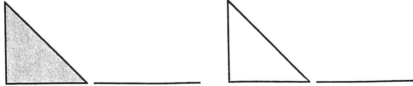

PIZZA NIGHT

Name: _____

Directions:

You and your family have ordered one extra-large pizza for supper. The pizza is cut into 18 slices. How many slices will you get if everyone gets the same amount? Show and tell your work.

There are _____ members in my family.

I will get _____ slices of pizza.

PROBABLY FAIR

Name: _____

Directions:

   When you play a game with a spinner, you usually have an equal or fair chance of winning. Design a spinner for you and your partner that would probably be fair for both of you. Spin it 10 times and record your results.

   Design a second spinner that would give you an advantage to win. Spin it 10 times and record your results.

   Compare your results from both experiments. What did you learn?

Probably Fair				Advantage to Win		
Turns	Me	My Partner		Turns	Me	My Partner
1				1		
2				2		
3				3		
4				4		
5				5		
6				6		
7				7		
8				8		
9				9		
10				10		

THE SAME SIZE AS ME

Name: _____

Directions:

Use cotton string to measure the circumference (that is, the distance around) your head. Measure right across your ears and forehead. Have a friend check your work. Record your results. Compare your measurement with your partner's. Whose circumference is longer? Are they the same? Record your results.

Find someone else in the room who measures the same as you. Record your results.

Look around the classroom. Use your string. Can you find five people or things that measure the same as you? Record your results.

My head is _____ around.

My partner's head is _____.

_____ measures the same as me.

These are the five things that measure the same as me:

1. _____

2. _____

3. _____

4. _____

5. _____

SHAPES IN MY WORLD

Name: _____

Directions:
   Identify the shapes you'll be looking for:

   Can you find at least three examples of each of those shapes in your classroom (home or outdoor area)?
   Record your ideas in pictures and/or writing. Share with your friends.

STORY PROBLEMS

Name: _____

Directions:

Today, each of us will create a story problem. You will use the storyboards and counters provided to make your story.

Your story must match your storyboard picture. Think of a mathematical question you could ask about your picture.

Write an equation/number sentence that reflects your math question. Include the answer.

Be ready to present your story problem to the class.

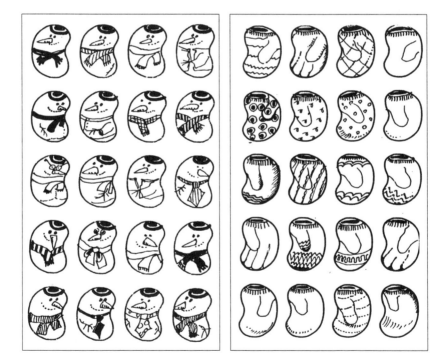

4596

Nyack College Library